A NOTE ON THE AUTHOR

The Torquemada Puzzle Book was published by Gollancz in 1934 and written by Edward Powys Mathers (1892–1939).

The author's *nom de plume* was Torquemada, a name linked to the Spanish Inquisition, for Edward Powys Mathers (known to his friends as Bill) believed that puzzles should be mind-bendingly difficult but equally rewarding when the solution was found. He introduced the cryptic crossword to England in 1924 through the pages of the *Observer* newspaper.

The British love a puzzle and grow very attached to cross-word compilers, always looking forward to the next week's puzzle, and Torquemada had many loyal supporters. John Dickson Carr (author of *The Hollow Man*, voted the finest 'locked-room' murder mystery of all time) was a friend. He believed that 'there has never lived a man with such a wide knowledge of sensational fiction. Torquemada of the *Observer* read everything that was being written… and was already familiar with everything that had been written. And he never forgot any of it.'

Powys Mathers was acknowledged as a brilliant translator and was responsible for an edition of *The Thousand Nights and One Night*, more commonly known as *The Arabian Nights*. The beautiful poem 'Black Marigolds' (a favourite of the UK's former Poet Laureate, Carol Ann Duffy) was another of his contributions. He was also a critic specialising in reviewing crime fiction.

In 1934 he published a selection of his puzzles under the title *The Torquemada Puzzle Book*. As well as some gloriously difficult crosswords, the book contained spooner-istics, verbal games, and anagrams – enough t

The final 100 pag

puzzle *Cain's Jawbo*

CAIN'S JAWBONE

BY TORQUEMADA

unbound

First published by Unbound in 2019
This paperback edition first published in 2021

First published in the UK by Victor Gollancz LTD, 1934

Unbound
Level 1, Devonshire House, One Mayfair Place, London W1J 8AJ
www.unbound.com

Text design by PDQ

A CIP record for this book is available from the British Library

ISBN 978-1-80018-079-6 (paperback)
ISBN 978-1-78352-741-0 (box)

Printed and bound in Great Britain by Clays Ltd, Elcograf S.p.A.

13 15 17 19 20 18 16 14 12

CAN YOU SOLVE TORQUEMADA'S MURDER MYSTERY?

Be assured that there *is* an inevitable order, the one in which the pages were written, and that, while the narrator's mind may flit occasionally backwards and forwards in the modern manner, the narrative marches on, relentlessly and unequivocally, from the first page to the last.

Please note: this puzzle is extremely difficult and not for the faint-hearted.

INTRODUCTION

In 1934, the *Observer*'s crossword compiler, Edward Powys Mathers, wrote a unique novel: *Cain's Jawbone*. The title, referring to the first recorded murder weapon, was written under the pen name of Torquemada. The story was not only a murder mystery but one of the hardest and most beguiling word puzzles ever published.

The 100 pages of the novel – originally published in *The Torquemada Puzzle Book* – were reported to have been accidentally printed and bound out of order, inviting the reader to reorder the pages, solve the mysteries and reveal the murderers. There are millions of possible combinations of pages **but only one order is correct**. The puzzle is extremely difficult and the solution to the problem remains a secret.

The Laurence Sterne Trust is interested in all literary works that challenge the idea of linear narrative (e.g. B. S. Johnson, Marc Saporta, Julio Cortázar) in line with Laurence Sterne's legacy, so the Trust responded with a mixture of surprise and delight when *The Torquemada Puzzle Book* was donated to the museum's contemporary collection, even though the solution was missing. After many months of research and good fortune, the Trust managed to unlock the secret of *Cain's Jawbone*.

Now, Unbound is republishing the novel in a paperback edition so that as many readers as possible can experience the complexities, red herrings and literary adventures hidden in the puzzle, and get down to identifying the characters behind the fiendish crimes…

THE COMPETITION

In 1934 a prize of £15 was offered to the first reader who could reorder the pages and provide an account of the six persons murdered in *Cain's Jawbone* and the full names of their murderers.

In the spirit of Torquemada we have revived the competition, which will close at midnight on 31 December 2023. Although we won't be offering a prize, we will notify any successful entrants by the end of January 2024. We ask anyone who is successful in solving the puzzle to preserve Edward Powys Mathers' secret, so others can enjoy the challenge of trying to solve it.

HOW TO ENTER

Submit your entry to the 2023 *Cain's Jawbone* competition by completing the online form at:
https://unbound.com/cains-jawbone-entry

The form on the following page has been provided for you to use when working on the puzzle but please complete the online form to submit your entry to the competition.

Printed page	1	2	3	4	5	6	7	8	9	10	11	12	13	14	15	16	17	18	19	20	21	22	23	24	25
Should be	—																								
Printed page	26	27	28	29	30	31	32	33	34	35	36	37	38	39	40	41	42	43	44	45	46	47	48	49	50
Should be	—																								
Printed page	51	52	53	54	55	56	57	58	59	60	61	62	63	64	65	66	67	68	69	70	71	72	73	74	75
Should be	—																								
Printed page	76	77	78	79	80	81	82	83	84	85	86	87	88	89	90	91	92	93	94	95	96	97	98	99	100
Should be	—																								

TERMS AND CONDITIONS

Entries received after the stated closing date will not be accepted. The competition is open to all and free to enter, and no purchase is necessary. Only one entry per person is permitted. Unbound reserves all rights to disqualify you if your conduct is contrary to the spirit or intention of the competition.

Unbound will not accept responsibility for entries that are lost or delayed in transit, regardless of cause, including, for example, as a result of any equipment failure, technical malfunction, systems, satellite, network, server, computer hardware or software failure of any kind.

Successful solvers will be notified by email or telephone (using details provided at entry) within 30 days of being named. Your personal details will not be shared or be used for any purpose other than this competition.

By submitting an entry, you are agreeing to be bound by these Terms and Conditions. Unbound reserves the right to refuse entry to anyone in breach of these Terms and Conditions.

If you have any questions, please contact
cainsjawbone@unbound.com

I sit down alone at the appointed table and take up my pen to give all whom it may concern an exact account of what may happen. Call me nervous, call me fey, if you will ; at least this little pen, this mottled black and silver Aquarius, with its nib specially tempered to my order in Amsterdam, is greedy. It has not had much work since it flew so nimbly for the dead old man. As I watch the sea, Casy Ferris passes with down-dropped eyes. Of course, to-day is the day. Her father reminds me of a valetudinarian walrus. But she has, I suppose, to have somebody. St. Lazarus-in-the-Chine is full, no doubt, already. I think she is rash ; but it is none of my business. Where about the graves of the martyrs the whaups are crying, my heart remembers how. Strange that he comes into my head so much to-day. I hope it's over some flotsam fish that the birds are making whaupee. But all the nice gulls love a sailor. Ugh.

NOTES

I plunged for the last time. The few remaining figures and letters swam as they came up to me. Then I took them in. There were no more. I glanced about me. I felt I was getting my money's worth. London is like that ; it accepts the wanderer home with a sort of warm indifference. The woman's beauty was, I surmised, profound ; her creamy dress, contrasting with her vivid colouring, showed to me, though more as white against a gay brick sepulchre than snow against roses. Yes it was a dreadful beauty, as far as I could see, and I recalled the stark phrases : Which swept an hundred thousand souls away ; yet I alive. But he was not ; the writer had strangely died to-day. And again they continued this wretched course three or four days : but they were every one of them carried into the great pit before it was quite filled up. Where was Henry? Ah, he was standing by her, close enough to touch the small buoyant face that topped her pillared neck most like a bell-flower on its bed. Would he appreciate?

NOTES

At my meeting with Clement yesterday, he had been quite specific : less than twenty thousand yards as average—seventeen thousand six hundred to be exact—full ration of the assassin's wonderful substance, a little act of justice at the end of less than a week, and then the glorious stuff galore for ever. I felt excellent as I took my second pill. At least I was on my way, for I had come upon the major half of a publishing firm ; they had always been very good to me, what with Austin Freeman, Oppenheim and Mary Roberts Rinehart. O my mother was loath to have her go away, all the week she thought of her, she watched for her many a month. And then there was a forgotten line. But the red squaw never came nor was heard of there again. I thought it a pity that Hodder was not there : what a sweet name for a village! My signs are a rain-proof coat, good shoes. No friend of mine takes his ease in my chair. I have no chair.

NOTES

And I really think I would have preferred the Maestro Jimson's title, now that this piled abomination is actually before me. But the queen can do no wrong. The rain that came heavily is drying off lightly. There, jauntily tripping from the edge of one puddle to another is crisp Sir Roland Mowthalorn, shuddering old thing, intent to buy the day's button-hole from gin-faced Annie behind the church. I remember clearly, perhaps because I ought to have my wits about me for another pur-pose, how Sir Roland's father, Sir Weedon, once saw Henry taking the part of Lesurques and mixed him up with Le Cirque d'Hiver. Instead of really explaining, she points me gaily to a little boy about, she says, to tumble into the sea. I turn my head, and see no little boy. Perhaps he has already tumbled in. In the snowy cumulus above the orange there seems to be now a hole. She tells me to mash all with a spoon. If she had said a mashie. But she is so beautiful. Can I suspect her?

NOTES

I hated my eye for being caught by what didn't concern me : the powerful grip of the new young man. But it was parading a couple of letters for all to see. Thomas Hardy had been, and my doctor uncle in the war had been just the reverse. And I would have to cut out the stops, I realised futilely, for something vaguely Buddhistic. He went on about Browning. I always used Bisto myself, and anyway Henry, the angel, was plying his intended fifth with Emperor's Peg—equal parts of vitriol and applejack in his case—at the top of the ruined lighthouse. I incontinently powdered my nose. He told me that, as far as I could gather, a certain good-looking Evelyn Hope was dead. What Hopes? I meant, did one know the family? It was really the way he took it for granted that I would rather hear him talking about Cerebos and Cerebos and Cerebos or something than attend to poor Henry that irritated me beyond endurance.

NOTES

I considered that venerable whose winter Achilles thought to take from the lips of Cressida. Why not? I set fire to one end of him, gloatingly, and my nerves benefited. Electric Febrifuge may be ; but bad for life's fitful fever. Its active ingredient had finally let me down. I was nothing if not generous. I started my fellow garden enthusiast on the foxgloves. He would appreciate that if he knew. Yes, I was doing my best for the dear girl. I wished I could make up (she would appreciate this) my mind about her. If we did decide—and that weighed with a girl—she would not have to change the initials on her parti-panties. I thought of the old spare-room in this very house, where Mrs. Gay used to lie upon her visits. When I was ill, I was put there, with the only dangling bell-wire in all the place, descending behind my head. I used of course to have nightmares of the Speckled Band, and awfully scream down the house.

NOTES

I had gone to sleep the night before after re-reading Typhoon. It had always struck me as a remarkable work. Now was the hour when Charles Victor Hugo Renard-Beinsky had risen untimely for the sake of the investigating judge. But the very phrase struck chill like the slap of the Firth of Forth above the heart, wading out over the coal dust in the morning. I had investigated ; but who would believe an investigator who had not stirred from Baker Street? I was a judge, but with no sombre little cap, and no machinery to make my judgements effective. I felt I needed something. Would I be comforted by a Jew's lime and the concomitant odour? I tried, and felt relieved. Someone had advised me, a few days before, to read Conrad in search of his Youth, or in Search of a Father, was it? But I had always found Conrad unreadable, as far from English as the Poles, and did not mean to try again.

NOTES

Could I be developing a green-eyed streak? I investigated the body before me with the aid of a powerful glass. At least I always thought of it as powerful, because I never could quite understand how it worked. I knew I ought to have the body as long as possible. At last I was satisfied. I measured the distance carefully with my eye : a good forty inches, I made it. I gathered from his talk that Guido looked his last to-day on the sausage place—furtively I knew how excellent—and that Kilmarnock and Belmerino completely lost their heads. But whether or not this was cause and effect I couldn't make out. I wished for the hundredth time I had a better brain. Later she was wearing the same bow—I loathed bows myself—and that time he found them and trimmed the left end. Then he turned what he was holding a bit ; so that it pushed its way right through. Then he twiddled the black knobby thing, and Mr. Hall burst in upon us. The knobby thing was black and red.

NOTES

The sound of the bell, as of a boding gnat, just came to me. The finger causing it was, I knew, the index of a most skilful hand, one I had commanded, one that would pluck me from embarrassment, and yet one I vaguely distrusted. Really, if the lower orders don't set us a good example, what on earth is the use of them? They seem, as a class, to have absolutely no sense of responsibility. . . . One had to be in the key for such things. I felt I should enjoy it as I got used to it. The bell again, and then a far sensation of feet. I was glad the man had come ; time was not unlimited. I remembered that, when I was returning after a fortnight's absence during which my assistant Charles Day had deputised for me in my lectures on mineralogy at Peebles University, a tactless hand had left on the blackboard : "Let us work while it is yet Day ; for the Knight cometh when no man can work."

NOTES

Then came Hyacinth's day. He laughed when he remembered that, as we were walking round the garden, and said it was too late for Jasmine's day at any rate. I liked to hear him laugh, and thought it was absurd for him to be called after what the man Boots didn't understand. The latter's way of expressing himself seemed to me childish ; why should we, of all people, use singular for plural and plural for singular? They went back two days and formulated their bet, till I could have howled. If he got the third point, she'd owe him a box of a hundred Egyptian cigarettes—Gourdoulis, and if she won, he'd give her three pairs of Etam dawn mist, ten inches. They looked so bright about it all. She drooped long seed pearl things right over the soup. Ear-drops, as my mother had called them, I never could abide ; probably because I belonged to the other side of the family. My mistress wore them ; was it for that that I had begun to tire of her already?

NOTES

If Henry had been there he could have told me
what to do. His great voice, tuned and broken
at the capstan bar, would have breezily put
me right. Tears came to my eyes. I was, I
supposed, an emotional old fool. So I came back
and waited in Orchard, it ran through my
head, where he cast up blinded that night,
which were my true friend Ravager, which
were always good to me since we was almost
pups, and never minded of my short legs.
Very emotional. But there was no need for me
to weep just at the end of the second dog, nor
would I. Henry had taught me a little of his
trade, and this, curiously enough, was what had
stuck. After all the Grundy Sapphic of yesterday had described a more universal taking off
in Ireland. I did not quite agree with de
Quincey that murders in Ireland did not count.
But perhaps it was an optimistic memory
which told me that such things used not
to happen when the queer old Dean was alive.

NOTES

I rubbed my eyes and massaged my temples with pronated finger-tips. Then I fumbled two aspirin tablets into my mouth : Noel Coward's King Charles's Head. I had a very bad head. My vis-à-vis hadn't a bad head, now I came to consider it, bowed over the documents. It is a very ungentlemanly thing to read a private cigarette case. I became a trifle abstracted. What, I wondered, would he have said about an abstracted will? He might answer to the same name as the man who sang : "Ah, are you digging on my grave?" But a softer fellow I had rarely seen. On velvet, yes, on velvet I would have trusted him ; but not on cinders, by no means on cinders. Yet the keen eyes bent like small topaz searchlights over the writing. I would get, I felt, what I wanted from this man. But then I suddenly remembered the words of the poet :

The golden one is gone from the banquets,
She, beloved of Atimetus,

NOTES

Rintrah, where hast thou hid thy bride?
Weeps she in desert shades?
Alas! my Rintrah, bring the lovely jealous
Ocalythron.

Then against a possible invasion of my privacy, I touched my white cheeks until they blushed. My luck was not in. He was a typical farm-labourer, with what they'd call in Bloomsbury a Newdigate fringe. Just like that sort of a poet, I supposed they'd mean. He anchored himself heavily, consciously waving an empty pipe. Henry was now stooping over the other body, whistling between its teeth. What would I have done, I wondered? Really this sort of thing was native to me in a way. I wished there were water without going for it. I remembered, of course, that there was a conduit dating from 1597 standing here in the market place. But that was of little use to me. On the whole, I thought I would have as much nerve as my dear hero. But one never knew.

NOTES

My ears were becoming attuned, and for the first time I heard clearly what the woman was saying : "Are you going to leave everything to me?" she asked, and I could have sworn her companion started. Then seeing, or thinking he saw, his mistake, he answered : "You must do just as you think fit, May." After all it was none of my business. Some fragments of disjected flesh still lay among the rests of the spilled wine. At my sign, Henry stooped and made all clean again. And there was no immediate call for me to listen further, for there came a pause during which both seemed busy with their thoughts. And I too thought. The voice was like and yet not like that of Janetta Sheringham. How we had laughed that day in the hay field when John sat on the buttered rolls, and we devised games out of straws, and we thought the cricket a war-horse, barded and chaufroned too, real fairy, with wings all right.

NOTES

Now, I considered, in my dear Lyons it would be coming of age hours, and I wondered if they would ever do that over here. I fancied what self-consciousness and preciosity there would be, for instance, if the B.B.C. ever took it up. A strange institution ; but the nursed fuse was always interesting. Yes, if sitting at the familiar table with Bart chewing at my moccasins, I could have broadcast it all, I would have left the mighty heart of England to deal with it. On that very day, I recalled, another terrible thing happened. John Hewit and Sarah Drew, just engaged to be married, were working together in a field of barley when they were both struck dead by lightning. Alexander, the only noteworthy Pope of my native land, was demonstrably affected. And my namesake wrote a letter, in which he said that Sarah's left eye was injured, and there appeared a black spot on her breast. Her lover was all over black ; but not the least sign of life was found in either.

NOTES

16

One's eyebrows were one's own, I always thought. Though I did remember a case—Aunt Mary's, to be precise—when it was not so. She had met him after the explosion, of course ; and when it became a question of dinner and the Highgate Empire, actually with performing quaggas, she put herself in the hands of the man who made up for, if anything could make up for, the Russian Ballet. And they dropped, naturally, like two fuzzy caterpillars into the clear soup at supper. The old days. The Highgate Empire, where Wilkie Bard, as Lauder did not say, sang o' his love and fondly sae did I o' mine. At last the two little horrors ceased in their shrill claim and counter-claim for sweaty quasi-transparencies of colour, and goggled at me while I put black to mine. Bill always called them two dark flapper moons. Should I make an effort and go back to Henry? He was ready to love. That at least was obvious.

NOTES

17

I am conveniently situated, with the Moon on the one hand and the Dawn on the other. Conveniently situated for some things, that is. Here's young Sawnie, for instance, parking his Fordor with a perfectly grey face. I'm sorry. He is fumbling with the lock arrangement. I've never tried the stuff myself ; bad for the hand. He's visiting the Moon for the first time to-day and just the first. I almost wish I had tried the Lapsang. I remember I once received seven pounds of Lapsang from Grace. Or the Moning, very choice, delicate flavour. Why go to pubs? There would be no Moning at the bar. Yes, there's Kate Somerset, looking actually proud. And that must be he. Poor child. Ah, here she is. She slips like a blonde lily into the chair opposite. My heart turns over a little in my breast and then re-settles. She is very beautiful. Why should I think her beauty somewhat sinister? Because, perhaps, marriage is in the air?

NOTES

18

I discussed certain passages with the man, and he was too guardedly ignorant in his contributions to our discussion. The chapter on the fall of the rupee you may omit. It is somewhat too sensational. Even these metallic problems have their melodramatic side. But would I have called him to me had it not been for money? Many a truth had been spoken, I reflected, as an epigram. Like something very far away in a great disused house, that may to the aching ear seem to be lifting a flag in some disused second cellar, my suspicion made an escaping movement, a movement of birth in a blank and distant subterrene of my mind. As I looked at him I realised that no single dish would satisfy the man. He would be, even to start with, for a course of soup, and then another of fishes, as my namesake said, and another of birds. I have never met any really wicked person before. I feel rather frightened. I am so afraid he will look just like every one else.

NOTES

19

Yesterday he got in another of his own kind,
who agreed she'd done it all herself. He
twiddled the polished knob and Mr. Hall came
into the room again. I heard him muttering
that it was appropriate the Human Comedy
couldn't possibly have gone on beyond to-day.
I, rather surprisingly, liked music. Surprisingly,
that is, to anyone who did not know that my
people came from the same place as the
McCrimmons, that famous race of hereditary
music makers. I was rather astonished to hear
him saying something about someone who was
by virtue first, then choice, a queen. Tell me, if
she were not design'd th' eclipse and glory of
her kind. So I pulled his sleeve. He pulled my
ears, and said it was Wotton, which I didn't
think it was, and that she had only just come to
Falkland. I made a low noise and at once knew
I had done the wrong thing. Usually he just
said William Sydney Porter, when I offended ;
but then he said something much worse.

NOTES

20

The best I had done seemed to me blank and suspicious, my great thoughts as I supposed them, were they not in reality meagre? Next day I would have to pay for all I had had of solace, and for all I would have later. It would, I thought, have seemed impossible to link Will's friend Ben with Will's wife, and yet they went off together, or at least on that same day : the bricklayer out of Annandale and the inheritor of the second-best bed : strange bedfellows. Underneath this stone, he had said, doth lie as much Beauty as could die ; but of course he hadn't been talking about her. Nor had either had anything to do with my waking, my strong tea, and my first pill. That all happened by the Mole, and there was the oldest brass in England, saying : SIRE : IOHAN : DAUBERNOUN : CHIVALER : GIST : ICY : DEV : DE : SA : ALME : EYT : MERCY. Good enough. We have circled and circled till we have arrived home again, we two.

NOTES

21

To reckon with Henry! That was never easy. Just beyond the laurels, I turned sharply and there he was, bending over the body of his latest victim. There was blood all about. I called to him sharply and he seemed dazed. Afterwards I brought in my rough old friend Calabar Bean to help me—this on the very day when I had proved digitalis purpurea, though I did not know if the profession prescribe it usually as such, a signal wash out. But why should this aspect have come into my head? Far, far from here the Adriatic breaks in a warm bay among the green Illyrian hills. Matthew, Mark, Luke and John. Read Mark Twain and inwardly digest. But I had to keep my wits about me. He pottered about with me and succeeded at last in making friends with Henry. Already he felt that I was leading him to the fountain Ponce de Leon sought, where he who drinks is deathless. And he was not so far wrong.

NOTES

22

He always talked to me about murder, when we were alone together. And that day he told me it was the birthday of a good one in prison. John and Cornelius, the Dort people ; I can't say I understood very much. But I liked his name, and showed him so, for he had always been very clement to me, even about that cat Jasmine. By the bye, Tusitala and Flora had both come over to our place. Of course you might say that was nothing to make a song about. But others had not agreed. And just as I was feeling how much I loved him, he put on funny clothes and went away. I lowered myself and made love to Flora. It was quite late when he came back with her. He had always told me that I was absurdly sensitive. It might be so. Explain it how you will, when I first set eyes on her I felt no vibration, no hint at all, of my latter end. I was banished and slept miserably with Flora.

NOTES

23

I hate seeing things like this in the paper. Bill
to Solve the Traffic Problem. Bill to improve
the Secondary Schools. I am never asked. I
am not qualified. It is all so sudden. I find it
hard to reconcile my guest with the Duchess
of that name, though I know how popular
everything to do with the Wimpole Street
singer is just now, except perhaps her sing-
ing. Toll slowly, a match box rhythm. Bryant
and, of course, May. Rub gently, she is here,
under the snow. Poor Oscar. Nor will the
ends drop off. Nor can her eyes go out. Pure
Francis Thompson. He sold matches. But I
feel I am letting the dear girl down. There's
a contrast : Fidelia Faustina Flora Blackwood, sister of Ebenezer Blackwood, which of
course it is. She marches by on muscular pink
hocks. The thought of that evening in the Left
Luggage Office parches me, makes my heart
beat differently. I must say I envy Alexander
having his first, and perhaps his second, in
there. I think wistfully of the poet's lines :

But rum alone's the tipple, and the heart's delight

NOTES

24

Of Cathleen, the daughter of Houlihan.

Next day I saw that my suspicions of Caroline had been well-founded. This was an infernal nuisance ; a Chinese confrère of mine might even have called it a hellebore. It was annoying to share the house with someone who reacted to wild jasmine much as he reacted to roses. He throve on my roses. To that extent I was satisfied with him. Puffing at Gianaclis and blowing at myself for a fool, I tried to consider my competence, or lack of it. I had always thought that to carry the name of fourteen popes and two anti-popes meant nothing to me either way. To share it with Giulio de Medici might sound more sinister to the uninstructed. At least the quality of mercy was little exerted, much less strained, in me. Roses automatically reminded me of my aunt Cynthia who had, before there was any constraint between them, asked the poor old Ahkoond of Swat to share a dream nest with her heart among these decorative but vestigial flowers.

NOTES

25

After all I might just as easily have been a literary bloke, like Jeremy Taylor or Eugène Sue. I told myself that all art was one. There might be superficial differences in their work, but they had, in the words of the old song, gone the same way home. When was it? Why, to-day, if I mistook not. I felt I must take a grip of my failing, in so far, that was, as it distorted the time factor. But in that case I knew I was right. To think of time—of all that retrospection, to think of to-day, and the ages continued henceforward. Have you guessed you yourself would not continue? Have you dreaded these earth beetles? But it occurred to me that to think of time with my delight would have got him guessing. I woke to the consciousness that I had done very little in my life. Not Dolittle but Didlittle. What was a did little? Didling, perhaps, or didlet. It was at the former that I woke to consciousness that morning.

NOTES

26

The girl had left Henry by this time, thank God. She was an obvious whey-face. She didn't seem capable for a moment of understanding those first two killings of his. He was being a dear. He had sent the rector's aunt away, as he explained to the girl, like a bee with a sore bonnet. A foreign touch. Killing *time*, yes. I was doing that. It was funny how idly the mind worked ; or seeming idly. Perhaps there was something in heredity after all. I pondered to its direction. An accent was a terrible thing, I thought. *Killing* time wouldn't be so good. I realised that I was impressionable, that I liked a good murder. But Hodge, once settled, wasn't in the least like a singer. He had a wen, and scratched his left whisker. I supposed it would be different to suddenly develop a wen for someone. Different and messier. He asked me about Ben Wade, hitherto merely mutely unemployed, and of course I said the right thing.

NOTES

27

I had seen, day after day, every sunlit or night obscured detail of the funny old house I had visited so many years ago. Through it, handsome, cadaverous and so quiet, had walked Death himself, tapping unnoticed at the very walls of the mansions of life ; trying here, failing there, lightly fingering for the sign of a breach, a tiny opening. Apparently the person who slept in the lock-up at that county town on the Severn, or perhaps woke, would hear this time. I had found that I could face my usual mixture of Peaberry Mysore and Blue Mountain. I had made certain havoc of two on toast, their silver skins laced with their golden blood. To think of the tiny Clem mixed up, nay, a prime mover, in such affairs. Useful, courteous little chip of a bat. He had hushed my brat for me when he was only six, one morning on which I had wanted to go out for a walk.

NOTES

28

I found myself by that one of the windows which overlooked the stone broach spire—a rarity in Kent—of Pluckley church, and the light would strike my book from over my right shoulder. I drew a volume from my pocket ; blind-tooled on the green in a double circle was a single star above what was perhaps a sea. I have had very little experience of it myself up to the present. I have only been married once. That was in consequence of a misunderstanding between myself and a young person, and I wondered if such a reason for marriage would ever have occurred to me. I had never married, and scarcely felt like beginning now. It was the tenth edition, of 1917. No, Sir ; it is not a very interesting subject. I never think of it myself. Not a woman had entered as yet. I was in for a ticklish business, and I knew it. Forging ahead, I supposed they would call it, since the woman was not yet dead. You might not hear of her again.

NOTES

29

It had always been my habit to rise with the lark, if there was one going up at about nine. A confirmed botulist, I first arranged with Flora that there should be seven of the long stout shapes rosily bursting from the exquisite, taut but not too elastic brown at breakfast. I trusted they would not taste of Flora and the country-green. Then with whetted appetite, and after an unsatisfactory visit to the spare-room, I went for a quick stroll among my flowers. If the West African ordeal beans had proved a disappointment, at least the broad ones were giving satisfaction. On that day—and indeed I was well inspired—I discarded my useless physostigma. I led the old mineralogist up the garden, if I may be permitted the expression, and introduced him to my lobelia and to my pretty lords and ladies. I wanted to see how the combination would suit him. I felt I ought to be drawing towards a close ; but one never knew.

NOTES

30

I see that the old dandy has purchased Cape
Jasmine. Your gardenia is difficult at a distance
to determine. It may be florida flore-pleno,
double white. Why should I care? I am a very
sick fellow. Gardenias! And there are also
Gardener's Garters, Phalaris arundinacea varie-
gata. I am not at all well. He is clutched
unwillingly into greeting old Mrs. Cave, our
local Dame Quickly. They mince at one
another. Yes, by James! James? Lo, how
these fair immaculate women walk behind
their jocund maker ; and we see slighted De
Mauves, and that far different she, Gressie,
the trivial Sphinx. We uncommiserate pass
into the night from the loud banquet. Sorry. She
urges me to the American mess. I wolf three-
quarters, thinking of Quebec. Then I try her
out, saying, with an airy lift of the spoon, this
savours not of death, this hath a relish of eter-
nity. Excellent, my dear Watson. But the leop-
ard's eyes do not bat a blink. Can she be guilty?

NOTES

31

The others did not seem similarly impressed.
Phrases of this and that came to half my ear,
duet by rill and corncrake. Rill vaunted the
pleasure of speeding, and corncrake gave warnings like an over-driven oak about to fall. I
remembered how I had listened for the same
sound on that awful night in Paris, when I did
not know what I know now. And again, in
this very place for another reason, Henry
would remember. To lose even two like these
two, swallowed by the night, was apt to break
a balance in one, to suggest that it was time to
square accounts. Caseus, ah! And nothing
lean or hungry here at all. A friend in the
nick of time. I would have no more. My hand
dropped to my hip pocket. I had to reckon with
Henry. Yet could I? This nomenclature business had often bothered me. Sometimes I
felt sudden enough, as if my head would burst ;
sometimes but triturative. Was I a bomb,
or only slow and godly and exceeding small?

NOTES

32

I was a little consoled for the weeping weather
by the fact that Gainsborough had gone out
to-day. And, now I came to think of it, Henry
had also gone to-day ; poor Henry, who had
stayed uncomfortably after his meeting with
Clément yesterday. Henceforth I ask not good
fortune, I myself am good fortune, I chanted.
Henceforth I whimper no more, postpone no
more, need nothing, done with indoor com-
plaints, libraries, querulous criticisms. But
that would be scanned. Or rather it wouldn't.
It didn't seem to fit. I had woken that morning
pleasantly near the sea, at yesterday's capricious
place of appointment with the man who gave
me my instructions and all I wanted beside. Did Wodehouse know it, I wondered.
Of its Earl he had said that he stood gazing
out over his domain, drooping like a wet
sock, as was his habit when he had nothing to prop his spine against. All I wanted
beside, I had thought. Hadn't Chesterton
said something about it's being hemp at
both ends? My job might prove him right.

NOTES

33

He was picking round among all she had left behind and found a box with his name on it. Also it said, for he read it, I always pay my debts. Unwrapped, it seemed to be a hundred box of Gourdoulis. I had never seen him so moved. He started reading a letter from a woman, dead the same day. I had yours but yesterday, it said, though dated the third of February, in which you suppose me to be dead and buried. I have already let you know I am still alive, he went on, but to say truth, I look upon my present circumstances to be exactly the same with those of departed spirits. I don't think he ever said any more. Happily I was behind the armchair. He just opened the box. I had never seen him so moved. There were little bits of stuff like black pineapple on the carpet. I knew he could never be his old collected self again, and that my gray hairs would go down in sorrow to the grave.

NOTES

34

It was a petty employ for one of my reputation ; you would not hear, I felt, much more of it. I hope you have not been leading a double life, pretending to be wicked and being really good all the time. That would be hypocrisy. I have spoken of ironic comment. There was, I thought, little chance of that. I wondered if he had ever been an innocent child feeding among the pantries. But that was no fit time for such musings. He took foolish occasion to tell me who he was ; as if I did not know. Bills should always be met squarely. I turned to the man, and his gaze soon fell before mine. He had always spoken as if his throat were full of jelly. Now with a leer, he emitted sounds through this quag which shaped themselves into hints at some perpetual reward for valuable services rendered. But even then I had not made up my mind. It was, I said to myself, a bad workman who could not play one tool against another.

NOTES

35

For the time being, Henry was drawing towards a close. I was not sorry. The police were after him in no uncertain manner, and it seemed impossible for him to ultimately escape them. While the flying squad had surrounded the house, the locals were thronging the underground passage, and Wellington Crisp, with his assistant and his bulldog, was pouring through the concealed panel in the bathroom. Instead of adding one more to his crimson list, he preferred to trust himself to a limping blimp : almost, it seemed, a certain suicide. But he might return. One never knew. At least my end was reached, and in some comfort. Murders were funny things. If he who so tragically killed his King, ever reached here at all, which is historically more than doubtful (alas, poor Richard! alas, poor Thomas!) it was certainly not in such ease or such good time as I. I collected myself and mine, and went out to sniff the new air.

NOTES

36

Strange that old Calabar, as I called him, should fail me ; yet on the morning after I had introduced him to the person most concerned, I felt certain that I could not rely on him. I would give him another day, and then. . . . It was distinctly awkward in a way. At eleven in the forenoon little Mavis Kitchener came with a gift of eggs, a clutch of eggs, I might say, looking at her determined little fists. Distinctly awkward : for, knowing they were bound to be bad, I spent an hour I could ill afford in finding her an equivalent in wormy raspberries. How could I marry her in the circumstances? Your good uncle, whom you count the father of your fortune, longed for this alliance. I remembered, as I wandered among the abortive Bengal attempts of the rhododendrons, that she whose bidding I then did would always make up. Henry was always made up too. He had buried the corpse ; only the eyes showed.

NOTES

37

Death's clumsy fingers, that was the really frightful thing : I had seen them, beneath a debonair smile, fumbling so long about their business. I realised that I would have to do something. This time, of course, the male incarcerated at the place of Hotspur's death could not hear. I looked across the table to the great brimming bowl of yellow jasmine ; young Alexander had sent them up the night before with an invitation to a private view of the Paulo Post Avorticists. Then I glanced at the rococo mirror on my left. Well, my parents had seen to it, soon after birth, that I should be one ; but I had never, save during that week in Malta when I met Ronald Firbank and was a trifle jaundiced, been the other. It was terrible to sit there with only the table in front of me, and to know that murder had been committed. He would—I had sensed that—be intrinsicated and concealed, chamber within chamber ; if I durst open the bores, who would believe me?

NOTES

38

I was feeling better already, and was glad that a memory, true though dim, had led me to the place. *Video meliora proboque ;* but I could not, for all my covert glances, see the modelling of the fossettes of the elbows of the woman sitting so near me. Were they, I wondered, like Sonia Gordon's, triangular dimples with shadow in them? Poor Sonia Gordon. I pondered on that tragic fortnight at Southend : the pier with its electrical railway, and my cousin's rash act, and Sonia's lapse. Her temperament was against her. Still you couldn't have an omelette without breaking eggs. And mine was excellent. "You would get off with a whole skin, would you?" I cried softly, as I stabbed once. And even as I did so, I thought of skinny old Marat in his slipper bath, the nightcap about his forehead, the dim light of the candle, the shadow at the door, the stealthy tread of Charlotte Brontë with the undulled blade. There was something wrong.

NOTES

39

She said it didn't matter what they had done,
because she was still an M.D., and she'd got
another one. That was he. She showed us
some delicate undercoats, all raw liver colour,
very lovely, and proved it. But she had, too,
a passion for getting new things, and I was
sorry for his sake. After all, in all my life
with him, I had only had one coat, and that an
inherited one. True, it was long and graceful,
and fitted beautifully, which was more than
could be said for some of hers. Combe, I had
always thought, was where one pottered
after rabbits. But there was a George too,
because he said so. He called him a Free
Knowledgist, though it didn't seem to me he
gave much away. He said this was his last day.
I didn't care. But I heard them say they were
two all for that year ; she said one of his was
vicarious and I could not understand what
the vicar had to do with it. They made a bet.

NOTES

40

What chemistry! That the winds are really not infectious. Now that I was approaching journey's end, I began to ask myself disconcerting questions. It would be terrible if she turned out to be Flecker's one. And some to Flecker turn to pray, and I toward thy bed. But I had probably got it wrong. Yet it was all right. Her spelling was different and it was long ago. Yes, but supposing she came of the family of Jack's visitor, with Thornhill, who promised the opera? I could never be sure of that. I took a pill. But it was worth it. Yes, it was worth it. The bean bursts noiselessly through the mould in the garden. He certainly could put that sort of thing over, the dear old bean. Out of its little hill faithfully rise the potato's dark green leaves. Thames Ditton's sister, as Eric Parker calls her—and one remembered the Irishman's malapropism in the same tale—had soon passed. Long she was ; but I did not linger to pay court to her.

NOTES

41

And then with horrid clearness I had seen a woman—not actually, if I could trust myself, there ; but aiming, directing, inspiring : slim, tawny, petulant, self-willed : wanton, but too calculated to be more than mistress of herself ; the kind that had made England terribly at sea. I looked back on my own youth ; I had been about a bit, as they say ; sometimes, to catch a whale, I had cast a sprat over the windmill. But it was not till my marriage with Henry that old Charles Goodfellow dared to hint that I was going gay. Poor lonely little Bat. But it was still the first dog, I couldn't help realising that, after my husband's training. Just as I could not help realising that, had I a mind to go there, I could now get moled and isled on the Selfridge side, though by no means in Bond Street. When I said means, I meant of course lawful ones. Then I remembered Henry's favourite quotation :

> But M'Cullough 'e wanted cabins with marble
> and maple and all
> And Brussels an' Utrecht velvet, and bath and a
> Social Hall

NOTES

42

Just broken to twine round thy harp-strings, as if
no wild beat
Were now raging to torture the desert! Then I,
as was meet . . .

I assure you I had not seen her enter ; but suddenly I was electrically aware that she was sitting near me. What could come next? I had let Henry guide me. She was very tall ; sometimes, I think, tallness is an excellent thing in women. Julienne? Yes, she looked as if her name would be of the sort. And I surmised dark eyes under golden lashes. I hardly liked to disturb the surface for the first time. Her voice purred in my quick ears ; I thought of a jaguar on a lean bough, and envied Henry. The surface was clear brown, and I discerned white figures within ; stars, and a little heart, *mirabile dictu*, were moving inside. She lit a cigarette and poured down cocktail after cocktail ; sometimes she made little dabbings with a butterfly of white lace to her mouth.

NOTES

43

This is good. She accepts Lover's Delight from me. She has spoken very little ; but she urges me to make trial of a Banana Split. Is there some esoteric meaning behind the titles? Now Ecky passes over to the Dawn. Alexander's my name. They ca'd me Ecky when I was a boy. Eh, Ecky! ye're a awfu' old man. Emotional stuff. Anyway Ecky has disappeared in the Dawn. I almost wish I took it. The hard stuff, I mean ; but it would ruin my hand. Where would my income be if Aquarius were to turn Gemini? She tells me a lot, each word huskily lisping over that rounded petulant vermilion lower lip, of a doctor friend of hers. I have only known her a few minutes ; but I hate to think she would change—her voice hits a pocket, just like a plane, when she talks of him—an honest station between King's Cross and Edinburgh for—what is it?—being's drone pipe, whose nostril turns to blight the shrivelled stars and thicks the lusty breathing of the sun.

NOTES

44

I sometimes wish, and I wished then, that I had the gift of telling, or at least of following, a story vividly. Hodge, in the luxury of his first St. Bruno, kept on exacerbating the corner of my eye by fingering his sebaceous arrangement. And this made it difficult to adequately appreciate Henry's problem. Smells meant a lot to me ; I was back in a twinkling at the old fonda in Vera Cruz, and almost saw the young fruit merchant laying down his guitar and wiping the blood off the strings with a kenspeckle handkerchief. But I must, I felt, at all costs get back to Henry. The position was this : the second wife's brother had begun to suspect. He had found a half-burned marriage certificate in the incinerator ; that was charred lines on Henry. What would he do? We couldn't stop at this point, surely, I thought. But I was wrong.

NOTES

45

It was when that half Pole, half Frenchman, and usually up the first half, that self-styled drunken mongrel and lazy waster, got normally out of bed. I remembered that when Hélène told him of her attachment he gave up brandy. And took to absinthe. It was one of the times that he had an absinthe. They said that it made the heart grow fonder. What had I actually seen? I had seen Henry—surely I had heard him called so—bending innocently over an innocent corpse of his own making. And I had also seen the doctor leading the old man up the garden, not once or twice, but many times. The girl was no longer there. I stayed myself with devilled Epicam and Royans aux Achard, levered into me with Peter Barleys and washed down and out, foul thought, with Villa-cabras. But one was so helpless alone in a great building of many flats : I was glad I had not given up stealing at the doors.

NOTES

46

In one way, of course, I was glad they were married. I had always been rather a stickler for purity in family life. That scandalous rumour of a Maltese landing on our island and seducing an ancestress of mine—or was it an ancestor?—from the path of duty, I never had and never would believe. If I had had a real education, instead of just listening to him, I could have told—it was bad that day—how I detested being called Hal. It was she that did it. But he was pleased in a way, and said to her, out of a book, the original ground of the transaction appears to have been sentimental : "He was my friend," says the murderous doctor ; "he was dear to me." Some Tom, not the one I killed in the matter of Jasmine, had done that, I gathered. He was enthusiastic and provided a chop for me, and said it was good he had visited England to-day for the first time.

NOTES

47

Babs now moves across the vision, crowned with two straight downfalls, as it were, of copper upon her head. The uncurling flow is to right and left, as if a river, reflecting a thunder sunset, had split in terror into twin cataracts. And here, thank heaven, comes the first, much needed rain of the week. A greyness and a spray to begin with, and suddenly a birth of little silver frogs all along the road. We were sitting in the verandah in the dead, hot, close air, gasping and praying that the black-blue clouds would let down and bring the cool. I always think of that, even in England. But, looking across at the figure opposite me, I realise that it is actually she and not Babs that has got me. Got me, that is a terrible conjunction of two little words ; Henry does not like it at all. But as a proof that what I say is true, she is strong enough to wean me from my thoughts of Orange Pekoe to a Special Orange Supreme.

NOTES

48

I had always thought that Tate essentially meant sugar. This I liked almost next to anything, though mostly not at once, but under the gas fire and pulled out when there was nobody else. But he said to her, as in the game a lot of them played there once, another had begun to-day, and had wormed his way into the Book of Common Prayer. But I didn't think he would taste so good ; I preferred the sugar one. I thought they were together much too much. I became convinced that I must be a sad dog ; I tried to remember all the times when one of the other sex had preoccupied me, and we had been oblivious of all else. I tried to forgive. He called her Crataegus Oxyacantha over the cocktails ; that was his big joke. I knew it by the way he laughed, and I too rolled about. But I liked the real way to call her best. I met Ecky that evening, he was very happy ; but just about all in. When I greeted him he nearly fell on my nose.

NOTES

49

I always feel a bit dazed on these occasions, and was so then. But it was pleasant to collect oneself, and count one's burdens—above and beneath, and to one's hand as it were. I did so. Yet I felt dazed. As I have said, I always did. I was developing a bit of a yen for Henry, though this was my first introduction to him. I am a simple soul, and I must confess that I was rather thrilled. It seemed that here was a man of no ordinary fascination, with a chin cleft like the toe-cap of a satyr's boot, and a little group of showy hairs behind each ear. Also he was doomed to destroy, for family reasons, and to keep on destroying. And I was still alone ; I could hardly expect otherwise in the circumstances. I echoed the words of the poet :

Bring Palamabron, horned priest, skipping upon
the mountains,
And silent Elynittria, the silver-bowèd queen,

NOTES

50

The swallow, the bright Homonoea.

I wondered if I should succeed in hurting the
girl. But think of her no more. The will was there
all right. And the wonderful hands at the opposite side of the table were at work with a caseful
of strange pens. I sat quite still ; neither in life
nor letters will I consent to jump about. I
begin at the beginning, even if you think it
prosy of me to say so, and go straight through
to the end. To be born, or at any rate bred, in
a handbag, whether it had handles or not,
seems to me to display a contempt for the
ordinary decencies of family life that reminds
one of the worst excesses of the French Revolu-
tion. The man had certainly got into his stride
at last. The fellow seemed absorbed. It is
a marvellous gift, I always think. He could
undoubtedly have written, if he'd had a
mind, like a Chesterton or a Camoens.

NOTES

51

As I was not staying, but only passing through, I raised my hat to the eleven that played All England for a thousand guineas, and beat them twenty-nine times in ten years. I paid respect also to a couple of exceptionally large yews. After all, I was doing another man's work for him. As I progressed, I began to remember what my favourite author had called him. He had called him lovely and soothing, and delicate. He had called him cool-enfolding and a dark mother. From me to thee, he had said, glad serenades, dances for thee I propose saluting thee. Also vast and well-veil'd. But somehow I had my doubts. I sat on the grass, and counted a distinct ninety between each beat of my heart. I would have to go slow. Each beat, I saw, puffed out of my breast like purple smoke from an exhaust. I dance with the dancers and drink with the drinkers. The echoes ring with our indecent calls, I pick out some low person for my dearest friend.

NOTES

52

The cardinal was acquitted to-day of all complicity in the affair of the Queen's diamond necklace. How quickly the quicksands of crime got hold of the mind's feet. At that moment it seemed incredible that I had ever been an innocent child, gambolling among the daisies, and thinking, if I thought of it at all, that the grave would be as little as my bed. The door opened and shut. From what I already knew of the man who entered, I should have supposed cleaner limbs and an air more sinister. I explained my object, and told him to sit down and make himself comfortable with the papers. Coffee and sandwiches of Westphalian ham pleased him too obviously. Why cucumber sandwiches? Why such reckless extravagance in one so young? Yes, I felt, at my first sight of him, that the words before my eyes would form some sort of commentary, ironic perhaps, page after page, till the end of my interview, and even after.

NOTES

53

So far the mind had been ambling, if I may dare the expression ; moving forward ungainly, as if by one hemisphere at a time. But now I keenly wondered how we should agree, myself and this well-fed swine that had just been introduced to me. He was obviously in drink, and none the worse for that : the better indeed for my purpose. The old fellow's face seemed vaguely familiar, though I am not good at faces. Suddenly I remembered that white beard which jutted from his chin like an under-curving wave. It should have been recognisable a mile off, from weekly reminders in the more ecstatic newspapers, as that of Sir Paul Trinder, whose *furor loquendi* had caused him for twenty years to adhere loudly to every ebbing cause in town. He was also, if I mistook not, some sort of chartered lecturer at obscure seats, one might almost call them stools, of learning. Such a man, it might be argued, was no one's enemy but his own ; but, oh, what a bitter enmity that could be.

NOTES

54

I was feeling about as good as man could feel that day. Everything horticultural, in the awful and literal sense of the word, was lovely. Green blood, as I considered even before breakfast, I delighted to conserve. I received a letter from Miss Doncaster, over the crumbs of toast and the last clear smear of marmalade, telling me that the old man would be coming to-day, on her advice, to take mine. I admit that she had stirred me strangely. I lit a Nestor and considered her letter once more. To pestle a poisoned poison behind his crimson lights. That was a nice thing to ask of a comparative stranger. It would have to be scanned. Poor old man ; but everyone must bump up against his Waterloo, and to-day was the day of the meeting at La Belle Alliance. It was not inappropriate.

NOTES

55

The picture of the Old Mill at Bramley, with its medlar tree overhanging the water, its octagonal brick dovecot, and its sweet water grape vine, had not detained me the day before. I had groped for my first cigarette of the day, eyes hardly open, a few miles on. So easily were things forgotten! I found it difficult to realise that to-day had once been an English holiday, like that other fifth, and for much the same reason. James had got off, the Earl and his brother Alexander had emphatically not. But the whole thing was not clear to me, and I doubted if it was to anyone. The two smells, of the medlar and the vine, had been the two notes of a chord, venetian red and peridot, that bit one ear gently and the other hard—or did I mean loud and tenuous?—a mono-tone save for this variation : once it had been hard, gentle, hard, hard, gentle, gentle, gentle hard. It had been a pretty smell.

NOTES

56

It was just when the girl from the Asolo silk mills contended that morning was. There was something, I reflected, about the fashion, beastly, in the awful and literal sense of the word, as of equals, in which youth treated the young day. Heaven knew I would have been in bed, had not my head been surcharged with too perilous a stuff for sleep. I spent those six hours in an agony of recapitulation. Even as a tiny toddler, at old Mrs. Larkin's school, when I was technically a mixed infant, I had shown signs of possessing these uncanny powers. In fact Mrs. Larkin might have called me Clare, so both voyant and audient was I. For a long time I sat and mused, looking into vacancy across the table. Gradually a realisation came to me that I would re-visualise more connectedly on an assuaged stomach. I hoped for breakfast soon, nor was I to be disappointed. There was that silly girl of mine bursting into pang in the sausage, just like Pippa, as she always did.

NOTES

57

It seemed from what I heard that Felton's meat had been delivered at Brookesley for the first time that day. I wondered if it was good and plentiful. Not that I really liked to think about meat, though we were alone again. I thought it crude of him to talk about no noise here, but the toning of a tear, or a sigh of such as bring cowslips for her covering, until I realised that he was thinking that Ben's friend had been, in point of time, like Felton's meat. Over the Westphalian ham, which I contrived to share, he read bits of paper about Hilary and the Amazon, and Stella Polaris and Voltaire, and the City of Nagpur, and Vandyck, and other lovely people. I wondered if he wasn't thinking of going on a holiday. It seemed a pity to me ; so unnecessary, just then. I knew nothing at all about boats. Some of my people had known the old Armadale Castle well enough, doubtless ; but that wasn't the boat that went to South Africa.

NOTES

58

Considering it was my name month, I wasn't having too much luck. Henry, though a bit on the spectacular side—to fly the viscera of his third, of the old family lawyer, at his small flagstaff, a little argued the exhibitionist—was sane enough. And this stranger, to judge by the over-vague conversation he began to force on me—different in this from the agriculturist, who had been utterly silent save for the burning question, and the brats who had only uttered mutually—was distinctly nuts. Nuts in May, how Freudian. Be not a Freud ; thy help is near. But was it? Henry was in desperate case, and this other was short-sighted enough not to realise that I should care. The former was stooping over the cooling remains of his fourth—the rash intruding charlady—when there came a horribly official knock at the little blue door. (Was it Inspector Barraclough, or only some stolid-witted local?) But little the latter cared. He went on talking about Browning.

NOTES

59

What was it I held in my fingers? Looked
at in one way it could just be a kea. I would
give the bird a phoenix chance. I lit a match,
and the consequences soothed me. Who was
afraid of the big bad wolf? No one, it seemed.
His silly bane had now definitively failed. I
put, at *petit déjeuner*, the cast-iron old object
on Gelsemium semper-virens. By the by, I
had a visit on that day from a detective-
sergeant about a poor fellow who had died
strangely. My slight experience of detective-
sergeants is that they have a manner ; but no
plural. If you use a word of more than two
syllables to them they think you are laughing
at them. They are, to that extent, acute.
Still it was awkward with Trinder about.
It pleasured me, however, I must confess, to
think that I was in a position, though the
opportunity was unlikely, to entertain di-
vine Xenocrate with an account of it all.

NOTES

60

I had sufficient knowledge to realise that I had succeeded. I ordered Charles to spare no expense in confecting that Sundae known as Lover's Delight for my companion. I believed in letting a man have a bit in. A couple of hours later the parson in the pulpit had, with his collaborator, done the trick. I looked down on what I had accomplished. Death closes all : but something ere the end, some work of noble note, may yet be done. That figure-head beard would plough the pseudo-scientific seas no more, at least. There had been other murders, of course, to-day, and with greater consequence. Francis Ferdinand's, for instance. But never one that had left a man more dead. I gave the huddle farewell, and forbade Henry, my peerless investigator, to pursue the matter further. I climbed down from the short flight of folding steps upon which I had secured my inevitable helio-graphic record of success. No more by thee my steps shall be for ever and for ever.

NOTES

61

I had always been proud of my namesake, the Great Lexicographer, as we, not unnaturally, called him in the family. But I wondered if part of my life would not rather horribly reverse his. After all he had been *born* at Colney Hatch. But no, for the goal of my pilgrimage might easily make it Broadmoor ; I rather hated that : portmanteau of Dartmoor and Broad arrows, with a little insanity thrown in. No, locked in, locked in! William the School-man—how like an old war song!—was of that place, and, in spite of Rysbrach's statues of the first Lord King, it was charming. Le couchant dardait ses rayons suprêmes et le vent berçait les nénuphars blêmes ; les grands nénuphars entre les roseaux tristement luisaient sur les calmes eaux. Doctor Invincibilis, dear old Bill, he was no mean psychologist ; he had a razor. There I saw a hen and two sheep. It was a pity about Dickens' insane jealousy of chickens, and one could really almost weep at his morbid mistrust of sheep.

NOTES

62

What should such a man need with such a companion, I asked myself. And then I thought of Jim's uncle, Darius Brockley, and of the flimsy excuse the Vicar's niece had given when she returned. Yes, I began to understand. And I was not sorry to dissociate the last of the gold from the silver, and wait upon events. I stretched out my hand and touched a dim shape on the chair beside me ; a sleek cat that horribly exulted at the touch of my fingers. We were told that the human heart was deceitful and desperately wicked ; what then should be said of the human mind? Why, I meant, should I have remembered the tale of the Major-General in Trafalgar Square on Guy Fawkes night, and how the dead man had told it me, just an hour before . . . they came to take him away? And then how about myself? Admittedly I was a warrior, but even I, surely, could be a warrior without being a bounder.

NOTES

63

I cannot help, even with this supreme distraction, thinking of my Babbie's—dare I say *my* Babbie's—hair as I last saw it, tiger-coloured, and all like the little springs of a fairy's sofa. O toison, moutonnant jusque sur l'encolure! O boucles! O parfum chargé de nonchaloir! Extase! If you take my meaning. *She*, at least, shows herself delightfully interested in Henry. I have always hated that these writers should be anonymous. What a tribe of them there has been, to be sure! But I have called them all by their names. Is it a foolish ecstasy to thrill when I see her long warm fingers taking off Henry's cap and putting it on again, and trying him out on the table? My dear guest accepts a Rainbow. I clamour for it, and it comes. She explains, and her throat dimples, that she will take it because Lent is over. She never, she adds, will have a second Sundae in Lent. I must be besotted, for I think this amusing.

NOTES

64

Needless to say I didn't know that that was
the last day. Afterwards I found it terrible
to look back, and realise that I hadn't made
the most of it, or rather of all the little things
that went to compose it, and the thousands
that had gone before. I heard him read two
things about a man and say that he had put
in his appearance to-day. The quaint, old,
cruel coxcomb, one was, in his gullet should
have a hook. And the other called him a
demure hypocrite or a blockhead. He must
first torture his postman, the bait, and make
him carry the letters of Bellerophon. But that
was too big for me. My people had always
owned allegiance to the McLeod of that ilk,
among others. But until he told me about
it to-day, I never knew that the Great
Lexicographer had tasted Lotus with him.
There was that in me which needed the
exercise of fealty. To give all—as I had
given all to him—was very bone of my bone.

NOTES

65

I started to read Hardy's exquisite production, and every muscle of my brain was enthralled until I came to the end. Just such another must have been the Monk Arnulphus when he uncorked his ink. His palette gleamed with a burnished green as bright as a dragon-fly's skin : his gold-leaf shone like the robe of a queen. There could be no slightest doubt. I would now be able to reap the harvest. And Ruth would have little gleaning. I thought of her mother and laughed aloud. All women become like their mothers. That is their tragedy. No man does. That's his. I could not help echoing Jack's question : is that clever? The Monk Arnulphus, with a dash of Jim the Penman. How, I wondered, did I strike him? I knew I should like to. His was obviously a slow methodical brain, used to pigeon-holing by type. In that case, I thought I knew the type : learned in a macabre way, even distinguished.

NOTES

66

It was neither sheerest hell nor uttermost heaven thus to affront the dead ; it was rather, surely, joy's crown of sorrow, or sorrow's crown of joy. Could it be thought morbid of me, I wondered, to sentimentalise a little as I sat and faced the old school colours frozen there before me? Green and white and rose, grit, wisdom and reliability, the fine old Head, as we called him, had quipped it. And now it was such an ephemeral combination. "I don't call that very terrible," she was saying, and I wished I could see whether she were smiling or not as she said it. Such remarks were irritant as well as stimulant. What didn't she call terrible? What indeed, with her Renaissance poise, did she, would she, call terrible? But I might lose all if I speculated. I attacked the viridescence in front of me, and fed my brain on cleaner things. I remembered the place of my initiation into so much that was glowing and splendid ; I remembered the clanging fives courts, and the solemn old Hall, hung round with

---

NOTES

the darker works of Beardsley and Felicien Rops, and ringing with the gloat curses of the Head, as we called him, lubriciously gasping in the grip of ether. I took the first blink of the light at the place of the Whympers. Mrs. Allingham painted the fish shop, I remembered, and the author of the Land of Mist played cricket for it till he went up the hill. I too had been struck from the float for ever held in solution, I too had received identity by my body, that I knew was of my body, and what I should be I knew I should be of my body. That was a pretty important day, for old Chris left Palos on it ; and you all know by this time the result of that. But upon my soul I wasn't sure how to celebrate, though celebration was one of my specialities. Ought I to allow myself another ration of my herb of grace, and sheerly rejoice, or should I merely weep? Helen and crooning? Poe and Prohibition? Canvas-backed clams and the prejudicial Menkin? The balance was too hard to strike. In the end I carried on as usual.

NOTES

68

Out cascaded the darling young. It was no tragedy ; that was, no tragedy comparable with the fire here in the Latham Chapel in 1906. Yet, I supposed, to wantonly look back like that buttered no parsnips. Just like reverting to old tunes after they were damned and dead : how often had I not caught myself whistling Alexander's Ragtime Wedding Feast in my frugal bath. I felt that Henry was about all I could hope to cope with, or with whom, if you like, I could hope to cope. I was the more fed up, therefore, with the incursion of an untidy fellow, a myopic-looking creature, who clumsily stepped on my foot and touched a chord of memory at the same time. Surely this had eavesdropped at my last crucial meeting with the old man. It mattered little enough, of course. But that sort of thing was like a mosquito about the ears, making Kreisler on his little fiddle. It distracted.

NOTES

69

I came out of my waking dream with temples
moist and tongue most damnably dry. I had to
believe myself, for I had never previously
deceived myself. Yes, I came to myself, if you
must know, when yon same star, that's west-
ward from the pole, had made his course to
illume that part of heaven where now it burns.
A time, I thought, not only utterly depressing
in itself, but also, when one is alone, as Dutch
as dillwater. What, I asked myself, ought I to
do? The answer was plain enough. When I
was ten I had messily collected eggs. When I
was twelve I had collected bus tickets and,
if I had known where to look for them,
would doubtless have collected whole ickets
also. The answer was plain enough. I
must—oh, final and most difficult hobby!—
collect myself. It was ghastly. I had seen
every minute of it. I had seen a poor old
man done slowly to death before my eyes.

NOTES

70

It flashed through my mind that the place between Eros and the Queen's Hall had horribly changed since Orpen painted it in 1912, also that even if I took the warnings of the Ming and got there instantaneously, my modest Munich would have to bracket, at my expense, with islands more correctly known as Efate. But after all I was not going. Rather I intended to finish what I had begun. The girl would find it in the morning, franked, and all ready to go upon its way. I had told all I knew, and felt very tired. Would he ignore what I had said, leaving me to do my worst? And if so, *what* worst could I do? Or would he come to me and cringe for silence, relying on our old association, when he had babbled at me knee, the arthritic one, that surely the cabbage butterflies were fragments of a poem God had written and, as being too good for us, torn up? Or would he simply try to do me in?

NOTES

71

But next day that religious fellow's head drapery, if I might thus unscientifically express myself, showed signs, it seemed to me, after that initial success, of failing. I would give it till midnight. Do not misunderstand me. Why should I not play the Spartan mother with emotion, be the Lucius Junius Brutus of my kind? I thought of May. Over them came old odour of red May. Lovely, indeed, but not appropriate. I felt that I was letting May down. As for the other, I had, of course, no intention of letting up. Henry, before our tea of anchovy toast and various hot dishes (I was never a stinter) riotously displayed himself all over me. He hit me once full in the eye, and I remembered, I could not help remembering, Elsie's difficulty when the young coastguard had tried to prove to her his direct descent from Herebald the Drake. "I will," she quoted, "express my duty in his eye."

NOTES

72

Of course I was sorry to say good-bye to old Medehamstede ; but it was pleasant to sit down and to really find myself alone at last. Those emotional times were trying to us all. I felt that my lips were paler than I liked ; but a touch of Pasquier's claret soon put me right. Dear old Pasquier, I had come across him in Paris, at that little place in the Rue de la Harpe, a street in which, I have been told, there was a touch of orderly room even in the disorderly houses. I opened a magazine and looked hastily through the last paragraphs of the short stories. I was all for love ; but fading out on an embrace never appealed to me. The embrace in my short stories—and my life was all short stories, I had come to think—occurred in the first few words. And afterwards the plot. The complete novel length looked better. It was called Savage Conqueror, and I liked that.

NOTES

73

All the artist in me flared up. After all, my
given name was world-famous as the inherited
one of a bold, subtle and delightful painter.
I was, perhaps, unreasonably proud of that ;
took a sort of proprietary interest in "The
Mumpers." Why not? It would have been
absurd to concern myself with Hamlet's one, a
thing of dreams only, or to have let my spirit
flutter around Runymede. But that was far
away, and instead was a quiet country town,
gabled and venerable, unmodernised and un-
ambitious, with a river, a Tudor ruin, a park
of deer, heather commons and, on the E. V.
Lucas a non Lucendo principle, immense
woods. O the orator's joys! O triste, triste était
mon âme, to inflate the chest, to roll the
thunder of the voice out from the ribs and
throat à cause, à cause d'une femme. I
rather relished my sandwich. But food and
drink were so bad for the stuff. I remembered the place of my initiation behind the
old Port at Marseille, the furtive plush, the
little airless secret rooms hung round with

NOTES

photographs of young and laughing athletes, lads who had profited and gone on, and ringing with those words of the Head, as we called him, that one by one the touch of life has turned to truth. But again I was distracted. "Will anyone know about them?" that husky miracle of a voice was asking, and I thought, not for the first time, that it would have caresses for all, a golden impartiality. To love her would be a liberal, no, a communist education. The red rose and the white only remained, and these were melting and blurring before my eyes ; my wretched eyes that could not tell me the truth, for instance, about that Goya reproduction. A hanging man? A countess? "There is no danger of that," the old man said, "I bought them secretly in Leningrad from a little humpbacked fellow, a double-faced Quasimodo of the Ogpu." This was difficult enough to reconcile with his Manchester speech on sane mediocrity. "From the secret police?" The words rang like tense half-crowns dropped upon marble. "Goodness gracious!" "But it so seldom is," came the wise old reply.

NOTES

75

I saw to it that I should be for a moment alone among the marigolds. Thinking kindly of those two other flowers, which I felt almost certain now would win me the girl I felt I could love, I exulted. Dear old Gerard, he said it was called Calendula as it is to be seene to flower in the calends of almost everie moneth. I turned the strong searchlights of my eyes upon the orange tinted documents. But I could not read them. My eyes, or something, were not good enough. And yet I was not among those who attempt, *ek parergou*, to confound *ephphatha* with *epea pteroenta*. You would have noticed my oriental preference when I smoke, and would not have been surprised that my Indian tobacco, after a scant four-and-twenty hours, was doing excellent work. It seemed almost certain that the blight would be destroyed : the blight on the May, or on delight that is as wide-eyed as a marigold.

NOTES

76

Looking over at the sly sideways smile which seemed to fill all the foreground opposite me, I could not help recalling old Lord Pentarry and his minion. "Tools must be tooled in the de Quincey sense," he had said, as he stood wiping the billhook on his smalls, over the welter that had once been so incomparable a lieutenant. I felt I could not do less. Maturity can always be depended on. Ripeness can be trusted. Young women are green : I spoke horticulturally. My metaphor was drawn from fruits. The Scottish nobleman had also spoken of a green stick fracture. Green was the name of the victim. Those little golden escapes, those logical thoughts, came on me like stars upon some gloomy grove, as Henry said. And then arrived the blinding realisation that if I did not do the thing myself— and I am not that type—I would be merely robbing a whirlwind to reap a scorpion. I would have to think it over.

NOTES

77

Compact, they call it ; but when I used it, I was feeling anything but so. Don't think me squeamish ; it was my first. That last little contact with the bony ankles, so warm and so soon, if Nature's great force were to do its work, to be so cold, had touched me, I confess it. Though I was alone again, it took me a few minutes to visualise Henry's predicament with the detached calm which it deserved. That old aunt of his third wife had turned up again. Strangely enough a jellyfish had plugged the solution of her motor boat's continuity. And there she was back again, alert, suspicious, very much alive. I couldn't help being sorry for Henry. And I couldn't help being sorry for Perceval. Murders were funny things. That day's killing of Perceval, and in so public a place, seemed to me unwarrantable. But I had never been strong on politics. For the other, my own, though it was understandable, there was perhaps no utter warrant.

NOTES

78

Then there disappeared the last rose slivers of
the Prussian beast. He had died to stay this
mimic artistry, and had not had an inkling
of it. The lips were wiped clean. He handed
me the new instrument, and stood half in
furtive assurance and half, I thought, in
fear. I felt I could afford to be suave. If you
would care to verify the incident, pray do
so. I never travel without my diary. One
should always have something sensational
to read in the train. But this memorial of, as
I thought, a soon to be dead woman's silly
wishes, now cleverly guided a little, by a
stranger if falser hand, was even more so.
We that did nothing study but the way to
love each other, with which thoughts the
day rose with delight to us and with them set,
must, as Henry said, learn the hateful art,
how to forget. Yes, I would have to learn that.

NOTES

79

It was that day my friend Sandy told me he was sure he wouldn't sleep all night. There was, of course, a difference between us. I couldn't get all worked up like that. You see, next day he would be allowed to fetch back Lagopus Scoticus, whom I knew well, and he hadn't been allowed to do that for such a long time. I was fond of Sandy and rejoiced with him. But I felt, I couldn't help feeling, that there was something wrong, something disjointed about my very front. I made love to Flora again in the back parts ; the result was satisfactory enough. I was feeling quite at my best, but I took Bob Martin in completely. After all he liked me to, and he was always right. But I had come to the conclusion that I loathed her ; she kept on colouring up. I understood why he had once said to me about something being as flush as May. Also she wore her hair in a cluster of little sly curls, a thing which in our family emphatically was not done.

NOTES

80

Hospitality, when I came to consider it, was indeed a funny thing. I wanted to do my best for this hopeful newcomer. My cellar, my library, my curious collection of bottled worms ; all should be at his disposition. He was pathetically eager. And at the same time, of course, I wanted to do my best for May. I showed him nearly everything, and he commended all he saw. "You do infinite honour to my little home, Sir Paul," I said. An old fellow who would be young again! He had only come before lunch ; but there was no time like the present. If it be not now, I somewhat foolishly said to Henry, who gave a slack ear to me, yet it will be. I am not incautious. Determining first to exhibit aconitum, I asked him to take a preliminary glass of sherry. Flemming's tincture might, and indeed has been, mistaken for this. He drank my health. He tasted love with half his mind, nor ever drank the inviolate spring where nighest heaven.

NOTES

81

The victim, for that I must now reluctantly call him, blocked all the sweet air from the window. He put out his hand and asked if death were so unlike sleep caught this way. Sed he. Death's to fear from flame or steel, I sickeningly gathered, or poison doubtless ; but from water—feel. Go find the bottom! He was asking for it. Was he to be disappointed? Oh, yeah. A babbled o' green fields (sorry, even in retrospect the habit is catching) which he could not have seen at all well. I pulled up his socks for him, and heaved outward with all my strength. The window was no more dark. The fool, with any luck, was dead. What had he said as he finally left me? It sounded like Quails and Arty and Fakes. Fakes, Quails and Arty. Band, Speckled. No, I could make nothing of that. But, thank goodness, I was no detective.

NOTES

82

I forgot why I was sitting and staring at the table. I felt battered. What could the batter be? Ah, I remembered. I had looked upon carnal, bloody and unnatural acts. And then, gazing at the steaming Lapsang before me, I became lost in reverie. Bartholomew pawed my ankles even, but I am not superstitious, to ladder danger, desiring sweet biscuits. They were so bad for him. He was the third dog I had had in London. I was afraid, I realised, that I did not notice him enough. It was the first dog I noticed, and at the very beginning. You might have thought it strange for me to say these things, but you never knew Henry. Whether as a human mistake or one o' the brand o' Cain, as the Poet Laureate says—and he served in both capacities— he knew his job. I felt as if great asses of mice were pressing down on my head, with all the cold weight of my certainty.

NOTES

83

A flower-seller, fed ruddily, it seemed, on hope, broke in and would have made a round of all of us. But she hurried away perforce without gaining her point, leaving me with an inexpensive memory of countryside flowers. Our own and other countries : ironic daffodils, irises of the stream, young pert bluebells, the foreign hedge-rose and carnation. No gaudy melon flower, indeed. Oh, to be in England ; how unquotable he had become. For I was, was I not? I must learn Spanish one of these days, only for that slow sweet name's sake. I paused to pass my tongue over the dew distilled by the red rose, the sole survivor, and made a sign which brought Henry cat-like to me over the floor. Here the old man dropped some metallic object, and his companion retrieved it with daughterly swiftness. The hoarse newsboys with their shouting of the late night final, as of accomplished *mal de mer*, disturbed me a little. Would there be any news? She enquired faintly what he meant by that stuff about good news from Ghent.

NOTES

84

I wish she would tell me more. I wish she would give me some hint as to why the deceased wished us to know each other. Sitting here, stung by those wild gold waspish eyes, I wonder terribly. I wonder dreadfully. I do think it is a pity. Auroral imbibitions have set Alistair on young uncertain feet once more, and he's handsomely taken the Dagenham bus en route for the converted oast-house where his mother lives. I hope it won't backslide. Barbara passes from right to left, dear child. Her one-piece is yellow jasmine, and she spurns the concrete and especially the abstract with those bronze legs of hers. The tawny curls of her are springes to catch woodcocks, and more than woodcocks. She waves a towel capriciously, take it or leave it, at me. What would I do now, if the other leaned across and said what the blind sailor said? But wiseacres contend that it was Kismet. Off went his arm to-day. Yes, what would I feel like? She is delightful.

NOTES

85

I was true to time. I had, it occurred to me, been something of an automaton. But wasn't I thrusting my head, when bent on such a business in this street, into the twin mouths of two lions, of Mycroft's brother and of the pale but multitudinous Blake? Often as a schoolboy they had guyed my name to a whiskified objectionable one. Whiskified objectionable was Kipling. And I blubbed with my face in the mackintoshes. But I thanked heaven that their childish jibe was true. I was still going strong. The murderer that is to be hung next day, how does he sleep? And the murdered person, how does he sleep? I only knew that all the weary business was ended. I looked across the table and saw that she was asleep. A nice old thing. I put Henry's keenness a few inches below the withered salt-cellar. I drove Henry home, and left him. A dog barked and mourned from the next room, but I could have all the stuff I wanted for ever.

NOTES

86

Next day I let Caroline Jasmine—what a name!
—do her very damnedest for my guest. But I
was doubtful of her influence all the while.
What a man! Henry, I supposed, was about
his business and concern, such as it was. What
is removed drops horribly in a pail. Why should
that stick in my head? Just because a tool
I have used, and shall use again, turned, as it
were, under my hand last week and said it?
And what more had he said? Has anyone
supposed it lucky to be born? I hasten to
inform him or her it is just as lucky to die,
and I know it. That should be, I thought,
a consolation for my patient. Surely such
a confirmed old tub-thumper would not
have had the wit to think out the Mithra-
dates inoculation for himself, and put it
into practice? Perish the thought, and the
fellow. Also my ravishing correspondent would
have told me. I found myself thinking with
a strange weakness of the poet's lines :

> *But we have all bent low and low and kissed the
> quiet feet*

NOTES

87

Of the old bold mate of Henry Morgan.

My guest has, I think, a Byzantine beauty, as of a golden snake. Is she, or is she not, a little pale about the Gills? Sanders comes into view again, seemingly improved by his lunar visit. He props himself and gazes out to the north-west over the water of the little bay, drinking it all in. I follow his gaze and see, as Henry saw when he was at home in Woodstock, twisted trees in front of the thick-windowed little house, and a foreground of exquisitely coloured vegetation with somewhat the consistency of fur stoles : a breast of the hills under a long cloud. I have given her nothing at all. She has let me see the original of the dead man's letter. It is funny, it is rather fearful, to feel a wet skeleton hand putting hers into mine. Why, I wonder? Not that it can really be skeleton yet ; it must be—worse : a loathsome mass of detestable putrescence.

NOTES

88

I always liked to listen to him. It was St.
Wigbert's day, I was told, and Augustus, I
remembered, was a chubby lad. I was getting
quite clever in that way. He said his stepson
had been misunderstood for a long time, and
had gone out to-day. He said his third son
had been crude. I did not entirely understand ; but I had a lot of good Tate. She said
to him. He said to her. The consequence was
rather dreadful, but out of doors. I had got a
little sick, too, of the way they went on ; like
that Tom and Flora's Jasmine. Perhaps that
was really it. They were having their first
quarrel, about the new distemper. She was all
for Dark French Grey and he for Egg Shell
Green. Yet I knew they'd get over that.
I had. But each, too, began to say things
about how few the other had done so late
in the year. I don't know why, but I felt
that mice were dancing on my little slab.

NOTES

89

The ancient had then sat down among the heather to a great dish of brown and swimming collops. Personally, as far as my stomach went, I could not love the deer so much, loved I not on a moor, with concomitant Spey Royal to drown the taste. Nor was that likely to happen in this case. The absence of old friends one can endure with equanimity. But even a momentary separation from anyone to whom one has just been introduced is almost unbearable. Circumstances, I thought, as I looked over at the man, alter cases. I would give the rogue a chance. "Have you a good memory?" I asked. "Intermittent but long," he answered. That signed his death warrant. Well, signatures were his business. The gold was being cleared out of the light ; the remaining silver was, how shall I say?, unsatisfactory. I also had flaunted the panache—it lay at that moment beneath my lips—to the public without ever having been satisfied with it.

NOTES

90

While my mind had been thus far away, a grotesque looking old gentleman had fluttered like a bat to the seat between us, and now deposited, with the bitter sang-froid of the unworldly, a dilapidated deer-stalker of pinkish tweed upon the glacial parquet. I thought I knew the type : learned in a macabre way, even distinguished ; one who was rich enough to remain unspotted by convention, and who yet reserved a thousand chariots in full force, gold of course, for the undoing of a materialistic world. Gathering a fungus in the other golden ruin before me, I considered within myself what such an obvious hermit could be doing among the brilliant lights of this notoriously *soigné* place. A dog was patently sorrowing in the distance. The two had their heads close together. The poor brute's howling bothered me, and I was glad when it ceased. You will, Oscar, you will. Whistler's jibe I had always taken personally. Was all my endeavour to be in the future? Would I never do anything in the present? It all seemed so fatuous.

NOTES

91

In my youth I had been worried that I bore the same name as Newbolt's admiral and Shakespeare's sergeant, and it had irked me when, in my student days, I had been known as the Smiler with the Knife. Afterwards I found it better in practice to capitalise my third letter. The Blue Rocket was still going down next day ; in fact, I knew too much to let it go up. It even seemed to be succeeding. The snowy-banded, dilettante, delicate-handed? At least I was the last. I would not say at last I was the least. I tried to interest him in my little Black Museum, and indeed elicited a *frisson* with the preserved eyeball of the well-known and respected Cadaver Charlie. The eye in which, just before its fellow was shot out by the Chicago sleuth, he had asked that suave detective if he, the detective, could see any green. It looked, though, as if Henry had been playing about with this exhibit. I would have to take steps.

NOTES

92

My earlier days had been so different. There
hadn't been the comfort, the sense of indul-
gence, or of adventure, that there was now. I
bit into the last of the oysters and someone
carried away the shells. It had been, as I say,
so different. Cascading down the bombazine of
my great aunt's knee, what futility! When all
her desire had been to give me a lap. What
frustration of her, and incidentally of myself,
when to be nursed by her and to submit to
her stories had meant access to that secret
caddis-hoard of Devona or of minty humbugs.
I wondered what Henry would think of next.
I had plenty of time, my watch said. My
eyes had groped foolishly at the barren
moon of the near-by clock, and then fallen
away. My watch must be my mentor. I felt
perhaps sillily ready for some sort of cardiac
revelation, or revaluation at least.

> *Yet now my heart leaps, O beloved!*
> *God's child with his dew*
> *On thy gracious gold hair, and those lilies still*
> *living and blue*

NOTES

93

And pipes for closets all over, and cutting the frames
    too light,
But M'Cullough he died in the sixties, and—well,
    I'm dying to-night . . . .

Had not the author of Wails of a Tayside Inn
said of them that they were the living poems
and that all the rest were dead? Had not the
singer of Wimpole Street said that they were
binding up their hearts away from breaking
with a cerement of the grave? Anyway their
hour had come and was now over ; just but
emphatically over, and I could not be sorry.
I knew, after arguing it out from one side of
my aching head to another—those little Bunny
and Perry, Pro and Con, had been at it hammer
and tongs on the centre court between the
two lobes of my brain—that if I had no
tangible proof against the erstwhile cleanser
of my old headgear, I had merely a thistle-
down of semi-conviction against the other.
That his thought process, when I tapped
its wire, had been calling her a Cambridge week, helped me, surely, not at all.

NOTES

94

Naturally I looked up. And I tell you I found it awe-inspiring enough to actually see my own name through the window, printed there in great letters for the gaze of all and sundry. With a blush I concentrated again on Henry, and asked myself if his recent activities did or did not constitute the darbs. With a final flirt at the fringe, the other tapped and scattered the saintly ashes. Agriculture was to take back her own, it seemed, and I rejoiced to have my last sight of the bent broad back. I couldn't think why I became suddenly aware of Yeats ; and then it came to me : we find heartedness among men that ride upon horses. It was here, of course, they commemorated Colonel Anthony every year. Good luck to him. Really I didn't like children. A little he and she bounced in, half settling on my side like sparrows, and devirginating a bag of gum prunes as they bounced. How could I concentrate? And Henry was waiting for me.

NOTES

95

I knew, of course, that if I got there in five minutes I would have double the time for my by no means suburban hops at the Café Royal, without insulting it and myself with John Montagu's arrangement for an uninterrupted session at the gaming table. I felt so much at one with Holy Mr. Herbert. Or Mr. Haddock did he call himself? But he was right about these hours, and if that was not holiness, what was? Meed kissing laces, surely he had convulsed us with. For the moment it didn't matter. Because I had decided what to do. Leda and Hebe, I gave my swan a drink, and then drew a sheet of notepaper towards me. I took up my pen, after having laid it down again and again, and, seeing that the ink was sufficient, plunged in. In clear terse phrase, utterly neglecting my contact with his infancy, I told him all, hour by hour, day by day, from the inception to the culmination of the horrid act.

NOTES

96

Now I think I will try a cup of what they insolently call Golden Tips, a fine young Tippy Tea. And then they say specifically No Tips. It is very disheartening. While I am waiting for it, and for the possible her, I study the only literature before me. What is a Loganberry Kiss? Is it at all like the Plover's Lunch, that hurts and is desired? It is strange to think that Catharine is even at this moment turning a Somerset in front of the altar. The whole business reminds me of the time we lay outside Jifjaffa, and the Padre said to me : "I would rather have written that poem than take castor oil in the morning." I had been reading him my Ode on the Intimations of Immorality in Early Childhood. Well, well. How vividly, whenever I adventure on stew now, I remember the stew we had that night. How it all comes back. The whole circumstances of this meeting are so mysterious. It gars me grue, if I may be permitted the expression.

NOTES

97

To have slept and to wake right up surrounded by an atmosphere in which Bunny and Perry went at it hammer and tongs, seemed almost sacrilege. That was the day when I was going to do a thing I had never done before. I looked at Henry, and felt a little sick. I took two pills. I had too soon—perhaps I did not want to go even so quickly as my ordered slowness—exchanged a tennis venue for a rowing one. I was not in Dorset ; but I murmured to myself that Ellen Brine of Allenburn would never mwore return. The connection was obvious. What a day, I thought, for the despatch of Paris and Leonidas. Cambridge or Thermopylae? But Paris? I had never at school looked upon him as in any sort a healer. I had, in fact, never heard of John Ayrton then. Ouvre ton âme et ton oreille au son de ma mandoline : pour toi j'ai fait, pour toi, cette chanson cruelle et caline. But I wasn't thinking of John Ayrton.

NOTES

98

He stood and looked down at me ; but I was not to be hurried. The money changed hands slowly ; for I wished to be able to describe him. He seems to have had a great confidence in the opinion of his physicians. I am glad, however, that he made up his mind at the last to some definite course of action, and acted under proper medical advice. But there were doctors and doctors, I would have to think seriously of that. And then he went. He went. Simple faith or Norman bluff? But that Douglas was, perhaps, less tender and more true. My heart dilated as soon as the sedulous ape had gone out from me. Gone, in a relative sense alas! not positively, finally gone. That was a consummation devoutly to be wished, but yet to be compassed. Whom should I trust with that? I thought of May. May be. May be not. Sunset was already reddish-purple above the Quarry hills, like a bruise on the breast of the evening.

NOTES

99

And she wore a mauve love-knot on her breast, and the ends were unequal. He said he'd put that right, but he couldn't find the silly old jossers, as Jasmine might so easily have called them. I was old enough to re-member her ; she wasn't the one I'd killed. He had read out about some most excellent potent brilliant eyes, swift-darting as the stars, steadfast as the sun ; grey, we said, of the azure-grey colour ; large enough, not of glaring size ; the habitual expression of them vigilance and penetrating sense, rapidity resting on depth. When she asked him why he had chosen those and whose they were, he answered : Father Fred's, and because it was closing day in Potsdam. I had had a dry shampoo that morning, a thing I adored, especially on the old chest. Rather a waste of time, though, as it turned out. Of course I ought to have been more careful of such a trifle. Suddenly I felt that I had put my foot in it. Still I had three more left.

NOTES

100

I dimly guess why the old dead so wanted this.
I had worked for him, Henry had worked for
him. If I could get up, as, believe me, I cannot,
I would have a thing to say to her. She lolls
over at me gloating, her mouth blood-tinted
on the puma freckle of her beauty. Why
should I think of Henry at this particular
juncture? I have it. Scotland Yard, of course.
And little 'twill matter to one. A sorry thing
to be last noticed : the buttonhole has escaped
from the buttonholer. He, the reckless old cock,
slips down past Woolworth's, and she continues
full-sail toward the Kursaal, as flush—oh, you
wicked woman—as May. The girl is smiling
at me. That's not so good. Here I shake off
the bur o' the world, man's congregation shun.
O beastly woman. You know not how ill's all
here, about my heart ; but I know. Henry,
I feel it, is for the first and last time getting out
of hand. Good-bye, Henry. He drops awa. . . . .

NOTES

Unbound is the world's first crowdfunding publisher, established in 2011.

We believe that wonderful things can happen when you clear a path for people who share a passion. That's why we've built a platform that brings together readers and authors to crowdfund books they believe in – and give fresh ideas that don't fit the traditional mould the chance they deserve.

This book is in your hands because readers made it possible. Everyone who pledged their support is listed below. Join them by visiting unbound.com and supporting a book today.

Jessica Ann Abacan
Mary Ann Abacan
Tom Abba
Margaret Addyman
Laurence Aegerter
Nicholas Agoff
Noor Al-Thani
Nina Allan
Julia Anderson
Mark Anderson
Maria Ann
Sandra Armor
Jon Arnold
Jennifer Asselin
Benjamin Atkinson
David Auernheimer
James Aylett
Paul Baak
Samuel Baguley
Simon Bailey
Derren Ball
Florence Ballard
Dan Bard
Emma Barraclough

Brian Barris
Chris Bartlett
Adrian Bateman
Raeanne Lynn Bates
Nicholas Batten
Carina Bauman
Ryan Baumann
Derek Beaulieu
David Belbin
Adrian Belcher
Richard Bell
Martha Benco
Jamie Bernthal-Hooker
Jennifer Berthiaume
Roberta Bivins
Robert Blackwood
Holly Blades
Henry Blanco White
Jeffrey Blomquist
Hilary Boden
Terry Hall Bodine
Christian Bok
Christian Bondoc
William Bonwitt

Meriko Borogove
Brenda & Jim Botten
Andrew Bourne
Alistair Bowden
Stuart Bowden
Bower Ashton Library,
    UWE Bristol
Luke Bowyer
Jeremy Boxen & Mei
    Chen
Chris Boyce
Jeffrey Bradford
Pete Bradshaw
Steinar Bragi
Jeff Brann
David Brawn
Hugh Brazier
Jerrica Breindel
Catherine Breslin
Sabine Brink
Stephen Broadfoot
Alice Broadribb
Alan Brookland
Jay Brooks

Antony Brown
John Walker Bruce
Llewellyn Bruce
Nigel Bruce
Andrew Bryan
Heather Buchanan
Mark Buckley
Cheryl Buell
Darragh Buffini
Ali Burns
Quentin Burrell
Skylar Burton
Marcus Butcher
Laura Byrnes Eggleston
Gema C.
David and Kate
  Cameron
Sally Cameron
Elinor Camille-Wood
Susan Campbell
Andrew Campling
Linda Campling
Javier Candeira
Anneli Carlström
Lucy Carolan
Max Carpenter
Joe Carranza
Melissa Carranza-
  Lemke
Dorée Carrier
George Carter
Anthea & Jeremy
  Carver
Nicola Chalton
Dave Chamberlain
David Lars
  Chamberlain
Andrew Chapman
Susan Chapman
Neil Charles-Jones
F Chen
Walter Chen
Conrad D. Cheslock
Jun Shen Chia
Danielle Christmas

Hazel Chudley
Alyssa Church
John Cirilli
Indigo Clardmond
Natasha Clark
Chris Clarke
Ellen Clarke
Theo Clarke
Jeroen Claus
Camille Clauzel
Barb Clifton
Rachael Clinton
Philippa Cochrane
Ian Cockerill
Nicholas Coffin
Elliot Cohen
Rachel Cohen
Katharine Coldiron
Joe Coleman
Stevyn Colgan
Gina Collia
Jessica Collins
Gareth Collinson
Kate Compton
Kipawa Condor
Riff Conner
David Cooke
Rod Cookson
Elizabeth Coombs
Mark E Cooper
Nick Corbin
Christine Corcos
John Cosby
Thomas Cottier
Kirsty Cottrell
Eve Coulter
Julie Crisp
Adam Crothers (for
  Helen Potter)
Anne Croudass
Lily Crowther
John Cruickshank
Andrew Crumpton
Jennifer Crumpton
Krisztina Csortea

Pamela Cullen
Richard Cullen
Heather Culpin
Emoke Czako
Kathryn Davie
Roberta Davies
Russell Davies
Sian Davies
Alex Davis
Geoffrey Day
Peter de Voogd
Alex Dent
Steven desJardins
Marion Desticourt
Stevi Deter
Nick Detweiler
John Dexter
Anthony Dhanendran
Jeni Dhodary
Jeremy Dibbell
Dallas Dickinson
Nikki Dillon
Andy Dobbie
Rich Dodgin
Stephanie Dolin
Antonia Donnelly
Wendy Donohue
Dawn Dooher
Maura Dooley
Tim and Jo Dooley
Imelda Dooley Hunter
Isadora Dooley Hunter
Dan Doran
Regine Dorothee
Ivana Drobova
Gayle Dubinsky
Gregory Dubinsky
Mark Dudley
Lindsay Duley
Léo Duquesne
Daniel Durling
Craig Dworkin
Dilys Eagle
Michael Eaton
Alex Eccles

Stefan Eisenreich
Henry Eliot
Meg Elliott
Enesthi
Jóel Enok
Thomas Epstein
The Erskine Family
Anthony Etherin
Stuart Farley
E Farrington
Jae Fassam
Neill Fearnley
Barry Featherston
John Felton
Jamie Fenton
Scott Fenton
Jody Ferguson
Francesco Ferrone
Trina Filan
Emma Finlayson-
    Palmer
Alastair Firrell
Robert & Jamie Fisher
Andrew Fitt
Stefanie Flood
Jamie Fong
Jeffiner Fornuff
Tom Forrest
Paul Foth
Addison Fox
Alexandra Franklin
Joanna Freeman
Christie Fremon
Emma French
Ned French
D. Freund
Andrea Friedrich
David & Jill Frier
G^2
Neil Gaiman
Jackie Gain
Richard Gain
Natasha Galilee
Ray Gallantree
Chris Gathercole

Sandra Gauthier
Leo Gayral
W. B. Gerard
Glen Gerrard
Nicholas Gibbins
Julie Gibbon
Elizabeth Gilbert
Michael Glass
SMC Godoy
Nicola Gooch
Katie Goodall
Megan Goode
Alison Goodenough
Jane Goodenough
Eric Goodfield
Jen Goodison
Stephen Grace
Richard Grafen
Sarah Granoff
Chrystal Grcevich
Amy Green
Todd Green
Joe Greenwood
Dominic Gregory
Mel Gregory
Sarah Grieves
Alex Griffiths
Andy Griffiths
John Grimshaw
Richard E. Gropp
Timothy Gushue
Pamela Hagen
Kassia Halcli
Ed Hall
Dennis Hallam
Jen Hallam
Stephen Hampshire
Peter Hanink
Oz Hardwick
Anthony Harker
Pat Harkin
Patrick Harkin
Darren James Harkness
Doug Harley
Hilary Harley

John Harman
Amanda Harris
Derek Harrison
Dr Hartebolt
Christina Hartman
Philip Harty
Guy Haslam
Carsten Hauck
Sam Hawke
Trevor Hawkes
Caroline Hawkins
Judith Hawley
Lisa Hayter
Jingyu He
Rachael Headrick
David Hebblethwaite
Cat Heeley
Ashit Hegde
Vicky Hempstead
Maureen Henderson
Paul Henderson
Rod Henwood
Guillermo Heras
    Prieto
Magnus Lie Hetland
Pippa Higgins
Richard Higgins
Stu, Katherine and Izzy
    Higgins
Andy Higman
Daniel Hillman
Bob Hitchcock
Deborah Hoad
Mick Hodgkin
Kal Hodgson
Camilla Hoel
Amy Hofer
Becky Hogg
Michael Hokama
Benjamin
    Hollingsworth
Erin Hollingsworth
T M Holt
Mark Hood
Charmian Hopkins

Carolyn Horlor
D.P. Houston
Pamela Hsu
Gavin Hudson
Hugh Hudson
Caroline Hufton-West
Hugo Huggett
AJ Hughes
Rebecca Hughes
Gareth Hunt
Ken Hunt
David Hunter
Leslie Hurst
Christopher Husch
James Hustad
Nigel & Barbara
    Hutchinson
Regis Jack
David Jacklin
Susan Jackson
Stephen Jacob
Naomi Jacobs
Neil Jakeman
David Janes
Mike Jarman
Billy Jarvis
Paul Jenner
Jay Jernigan
Amy Johnson
Timo Jokitalo
Julie Jones
Stephen Jorgenson-
    Murray
Erin Jospe
George Kaltsios
Catherine Kantner
Jonas Karlsson
Zara and Stephan
    Karschay
Christine Kassir
Rhonda Kauth
Ed Kay
Anthony Liam Kearns
Stephanie Keen
Patric Keller

Jean Kemp
Adam Kennedy
Harry Kent
Sarah Kerschbaum
Jonathan Key
Dan Kieran
Alison Kind
Chris King
The King's School
    Library
Simon Kingston
Karl Kinsella
Sarah Kirkland
F. Stephen Kirschbaum
Matthew Kirschenbaum
Lena Klambauer
Sylvie Kleiman-Lafon
James Kloss
Ashley Knowles
Ekin Koker
Peter Kolkay
Carol Kopaczewski
Andrew Kozma
Dan Kramarsky
Joan Krause
Mathieu Kudla
Marta Kvande
Evelyn Laing
Laura Lamb & Dave
    Miatt
Keiran Lancaster
Elizabeth Lane
Richard Lane
Robin Lasne
Derek Law
Gayle Lazda
Trish Leach
Roy Leban
Jennifer Lee
Fi Leiper
Lel
Aimee Lerman
Marilia Leti
Hannah Levene
Lisa Lewis

Sandy Li
Scott Liddell
Andy Lin
Clare Lin
Silvia Lin Hanick
Kimberly Linder
Rachel Littlefield
Virginia Livingston
Victoria Lloyd-Hughes
Thomas Lobinger
Eric Logan
Keith Long
Kim Melanie Lonny
Angela Lord
Gregory Loselle
Vittoria Lubrano
Penelope Lynch
David Lynd
Mike Lynd
Jo Macdonald
Nicholas Maggiore
Pat Mahony
Andrew Maise
Philippa Manasseh
Jonathan Mann
Malen Manya
Char March
Matthew Marcus
Christine Marlowe
Jon Marsh
Madeleine Marsh
Esther Martijn
Côme Martin
Jason Martin
Leon Marzillier
Stacey Mason
Anthony Mastracco
Autumn Mather
John McCallin
Ellen McCarthy
Kate McCormack
Melody McCormick
Pio McDonnell
Jesse McGatha
Anna McGrail

Clare McHale
Gavin McKeown
Max McLaughlin
Joseph McMahon
Paul McNally
Liz McNeil
Richard McPherson
Hannah and Mick
    McReynolds
Rebecca Meacham
Bairbre Meade
Alec Meadows
Aleksandra Medic
Kristofer Mehaffey
Joseph Mela
Hareesh Menon
Molly Merson
Esther Mettler
James Mewis
Georgina Micross
Jane Middleton
Clare Miles
Melissa Milford
David Miller
Mell Miller
Peter Miller
Philip Miller
Roxanne Miller
Christina Mills
Steve Miraglio
Ev Mis
Julianna Mitchell
John Mitchinson
Ronald Mitchinson
Ian Monk
Stephanie Monk
Penny Montague
Tom Moody-Stuart
Jess Moralde
Anna Morgan
Jonny Morris
Simon Morris
Rowan Morrison
Maurice Moscovich
Anne Vibeke Mou

Bernard Moxham
Sylvia Moyes & Sarina
    Hao
Joerg Mueller-Kindt
Robert Mullan
Maike Muller
Brenna Murdock
Joanna Murray
Jason Mutschler
Laura Naethe
Jon Napolitano
Carlo Navato
Tim Naylor
Sam Negus
Neil's offspring &
    partners!!
John New
Tiffany Newhill-Leahy
Andy Nichol
Irene Nichols
Jack Nichols
Timandra Nichols
Jeroen Nieuwkoop
Marie-Jose Nieuwkoop
Michael Nightingale
Angela Nikkola
Alexander Nirenberg
Bruno Noble
Andrew and Elena
    North
Bri Norton
Jim Noy
Penn O'Gara
Carrie O'Grady
Elizabeth O'Hara
Tony Oganesian
Jessica Oreck
Catie Osborn
Andrew Osborne
Quantella Owens
Richard Owens
Victoria Oxberry
Ryan Pachmayer
Scott Pack
Jon Padgett

Noelle Paduan
Sally Painter
John Palagyi
Laura Panini
Nick Parfitt
Lev Parikian
Clare Park
Craig Parker
Kylie Parker
Tim Parnell
Abigail Parry
Sheila Parry
Angela Patel
Nimesh Patel
James and Dusty
    Patrick
Sue Patrick
Andrew Patterson
Ian Patterson
Callum Pearce
Chris Pearson
Velvet Pearson
Tanya Peixoto
Luis Pena
Nadia Permogorov
Patti Petersen
Emma Pewsey
Roger Phillips
Tim Phillips
Gavin Philpott
Marian Pickles
Hugh Platt
Johnny Plissken
Susanne Pohl
Justin Pollard
Beki Pope
Richard Powell
Ed Powles
Martin Pråme
    Malmqvist
Christopher Pridham
Amanda Priestley
Jo Problems
Malin Provido
Laura Pullin

Chris Purser
Emma Pusill (Plum Duff)
Sarah Pyke
Adam Queripel
Brendan Quigley
Liza Radley
Jane Raffaele Krause
JP Rangaswami
Paul Rascoe
Joad Raymond
Charles Reams
Moira Redmond
Owen Rees
Vernon Reeves
Mandie Reinen
Sean Reisz
Rick Rhubart
Jane Richardson
Philip Richardson
Phyllis Richardson
Tara Richerson
Mathis Riehle
Matt Ritenour
Paul Jason Robb
Kara Roberts
Wyn Roberts
Anthea Robertson
Hazel Robertson
James Robertson
Simon Robertson
Adriene Robins
Mark Robinson
Vincent Roca
Matthew Rodgers
The Rodgers'
Dan Roe
Kalina Rose
HJ Rose-Innes
Olivia Rossanese
Max Rossi
David Rotheray
Anna Route
Matthew Rowbottom
John Rowland

Patrick and Karen Rowland
Alan Roxburgh
Sudipta Roy
Ian Runacres
Joe Russell
Joseph Russell
Paul Rutherford
Malcolm Ryan
Charles Rybak
Alice Sage
Lisa Sainsbury
Samuel Sanderson-Hutley
Amy Sandler
Marivi Sanz
Brendan Sargeant
Jon Sayer
Jane Schaffer
Dan Schmidt
Stefan Schmiedl
Matthew L. Schuett
Jutta Schuhmann
Dan Schulman
Andy Schultheiss
Alison Scott
Anne-Marie Scott
Gregor Scott
Michelle Scott
Matthew Searle
Owen Searle
Myra Sefton
Sue Shade
AJ Sharp
Jasmine Sharp
Robert Sharp
Saffron Sharp
Christian Sheppard
Laura Shepperson-Smith
Steven Shepperson-Smith
Jean Sheridan
Marquel Sherry
Ryan Shim

Anna Shinoda
John Shirlaw
Brandall Shumard
Jonathan Siklos
Joana Silva
Ian Simpson
Thomas Simpson
Andrew Sinclair
Susan Singley
Michael Skelly
Rhianan Skinner
Piotr Skorupa
Toni Smerdon
Catherine Smillie
Chris Smith
Christine Smith
Drew Smith
Lindsey Smith
Liz Smith
Nigel Smith
Paul Smith
Smoot
Smudge
Adam Smyth
Josiah Snell
Claire Snodgrass
Brenna Snowie
Jonathan South
Kerri J Spangaro
Iain Spardagus
Roger Sparks
Philip Spedding
Liam Spinage
David Spira
Max Staab
Johnny Stafford
Kirsty Stanley
Markus Steck
Peter Steggle
Rob Stegmann
Laurie Steiger
Alaric Stephen
Anthony Sterne
Robert Sterne
A. Stevens

Laura Stevens
Robin Stevens
Adam Stevenson
Bourgnet Stogner
Adam Stone
Emma Jane Stone
Pete Stones
Nina Stutler
Ryan Sullentrup
Gavin Swanson
Matthew Swenson
Jane Sykes
Jean Takabayashi
Cheng Tang
Stephanie Tanizar
Mary Tate
Stephen Tavener
Andy Taylor
Deb Taylor
Mark Taylor
Siobhan Taylor
The TBevs
Wendy Tebbatt
Jillian Tees
Veronika Temml
Denise Theyers
Kristin Theyers
Jan Thie
Darlah Thomas
Gareth Thomas
Helena Thomas
Phil Thomas
Steven Thomas
Ali Thompson
Patrick Thompson
Henry Thorogood
Olivia Threlkeld
Marnanel and Kit
    Thurman
Amanda Thurman and
    Matti Keltanen
Nick Thurston
Hannah Tighe
Penelope Tindall
Jonathan Tisdall

James Tobin
Rebecca Tolfrey
Andreea Toma
Bel Tomov
Samuel Toogood
John and Jo Toon
Garen Torikian
David Tosh
Jeff Towns
Adin Townsend
Lori Townsend
R D Townsend
Vanessa Townsend
Rob Toyias
John Tozer
Simon Trafford
Steve Tregidgo
Matt Tubb
Jime Turanza
Yvette Turnbull
Michelle Tutt
Alex Twiston Davies
Christopher Tyas
Lewis Tyrrell
Uwe Uhlendorff
Ernst Unding
Steven Valdez
Disa Valemark
FJ van den Berg
Tom van Heel
BT Varberg
JM Varberg
Sandra Vasconcelos
Mark Vent
Gary Vernon
Samuel Vimes
Nicklas von Plenker-
    Tind aka
    KingVoodoo
Paul Wake
Angus Walker
Steve Walker
Peter Walker-Birch
Ashley Wall
Ian Wall

Nick Walpole
Jennifer Walsh
Kathryn Walsh
    Kuitenbrouwer
Sean Walton
Gareth Ward
Chris Warnick
Julie Warren
Kyra Watral
Steve Watts
Diane Weaver
Steve Weaver
Richard Webb
Nadja Weber
Joseph Weeg
Stefan Weger
Richard E. Weill
Alexander Weir
Alexander Welch
Kylie Wells
Robert Wells
Alexandra Welsby
Anne Welsh
Mike Westcott
James Westine
Katie Weston
Sarah Westwood
Sima Westwood
Deanna Westwood MA
Colin Whelan
Paul Whelan
Colin White
Joseph White
Joe Whitlock Blundell
David Wickes
Lori Wike
Patrick Wildgust
Tim Wilkinson Lewis
Cordelia Williams
Helen Williams
Simon Williams
Lynette Willoughby
Fiona Wilson
John Wilson
John Winter

Vlad Wolynetz
Lynda Wong
Jo Wood
Lucy Wood
Katherine Wright
Simon Wright
Robert Wyke

Debbie Wythe
XFOML
Duncan Yeates
Samuel Yeo
James Youhas
Laura Young
Peter Young

Dale Yu
William Zachs
Johan Zandin
Robert Zara
Tamara Zavodska
Laura Zeilo